H23 626 959 3   PRICE, T.   The angler's
                                 sedge

799.1'2

D0349399

FA

THE ANGLER'S SEDGE

TYING AND FISHING THE CADDIS

THE
ANGLER'S SEDGE

TYING AND FISHING THE CADDIS

TAFF PRICE

BLANDFORD

Series editor: Jonathan Grimwood
Designed by Will Denley

First published in the UK 1989 by
Blandford Press,
An imprint of Cassell,
Artillery House, Artillery Row, London SW1P 1RT

Copyright © Taff Price 1989

All rights reserved.
No part of this book may be reproduced
or transmitted in any form or by any means,
electronic or mechanical, including photocopying,
recording or any information storage and
retrieval system, without prior permission
in writing from the publishers.

Distributed in the United States by
Sterling Publishing Co, Inc,
2 Park Avenue, New York, NY 10016

Distributed in Australia by
Capricorn Link (Australia) Pty Ltd
PO Box 665, Lane Cove, NSW 2066

British Library Cataloguing in Publication Data

Price, Taff, *1934–*
The angler's sedge: tying and fishing the caddis
1. Fly fishing. Flies
I. Title
799.1′2

ISBN 0 7137 2103 0

Typeset by Graphicraft Typesetters Ltd., Hong Kong
set by Monotype Lasercomp in 11 on 13pt Garamond
Printed and bound in Great Britain
by Courier International Ltd, Tiptree, Essex

HERTFORDSHIRE
LIBRARY SERVICE

799.12

DEDICATION
For my wife Madeleine, my constant fishing companion,
who has to put up with a great deal and still lets me
catch the biggest trout, sometimes.

CONTENTS

ACKNOWLEDGEMENTS

I would like to thank all those fly fishermen and fly tiers whose flies appear in this book and also those who gave or sent me their patterns, in particular the following: Marjan Fratnik, Dr Bozidar Voljč, Francesco Palu, Roman Moser, Rudi Rubel, Rudi Heger, Raymond Rocher, Luis Antunez, Victor Salt, Steff Steffersen, Gorjan Franco, B. Gasparin, Marjan Danush, Savo Martinovic.

I would also like to acknowledge the information sent to me by the Fisheries Research Institute of Ljubljana and in particular their Director, Jose Ocvirk, who annually allows me to fish some of their beautiful rivers and streams. My thanks to John Goddard for kindly letting me have the slides for the *P. grandis* and *O. lacustris*. My thanks must also go to Darrel Martin of Tacoma Washington State for his help over the years in endeavouring to teach me to draw and for not laughing too much at my amateurish illustrations. Finally, my thanks to Jonathan Grimwood who gently persuaded me to write the book in the first place.

INTRODUCTION

The birthplace of the stream was high up in the hills, just a syrup-slow trickle emanating from the soft bog; a wetness from the spongy sphagnum moss. In this place it dampened the sundew and wetted the feet of the snipe and curlew.

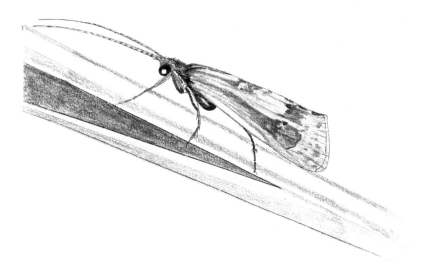

Small trickle joined small trickle and they slowly gathered strength until they formed a tiny brook. Over thousands of years this small stream had carved for itself a deep valley in the Precambrian granite; a valley flanked by moss-covered oaks and bushes of wild bilberry, where the buzzard nested and owls slept the daylight hours, where stray sheep went to hide and where small boys discovered new worlds. Perhaps in earlier times it was a much bigger stream, a legacy of the Ice Age when the melting glaciers retreated before the warming sun. The stream flowed through the wooded valley, a place scented by wild mint and wilder garlic. Small trout hid behind the stones and green frogs sat goggle-eyed in the green of the bankside – perhaps drugged by the peppermint or the scent of the garlic.

For a short while the singing stream left behind all natural beauty and gushed through a large, rust-red iron pipe. (It had been easier in those early days to carry the road over an iron pipe than to construct a bridge.) It next flowed through a park we called 'Fairy Glen'. Still alive it sang its way towards the sea, ignoring the fact that careless man had constructed the town's rubbish dump, a hundred yards or so to the left. This place was a mass of grey, white and black, as gulls, aided by humped-backed crows, picked over the waste like Victorian scavengers.

Soon the stream reached the sandbanks where it slid quietly between the mounds of shifting sands and close, rabbit-clipped grass. Once again it flowed into a large iron pipe, this time a pipe bearded with seaweed and encrusted with barnacles and limpets. From the mouth of this large pipe it poured its soul into the Irish Sea.

It must be well over 40 years since I sat by the side of that stream on a carpet of grass and clover, but I can remember it as though it were only yesterday. It was my introduction to the world of the caddis, or the sedge as some people called it. I can vividly recall staring in wonder into the water, marvelling at the tiny, gravel-encrusted caddis larvae busying themselves in the silt of the stream. It is strange that I should remember that insignificant stream and its tiny inhabitants, but even today whenever I see a fluttering sedge or a tiny caddis larva, I remember that small boy who sat beside a stream just looking at the insects that crawled amidst the gravel.

I would like to tell you that the stream still sings in the valley on its way to the sea but, alas, it is long gone. Someone has taken the water for another valley and another place, and the bare stones of the departed stream lie like the skeleton of some giant reptile, dry and bleached by time. Herons now tiptoe on the sphagnum so as not to wake the spirits of the dead stream. No longer do the caddis busy themselves in the silt and neither do the brown-winged sedges flutter above the sandbanks. They remain only as a crystal of memory in my mind, a small spark that rekindles, no matter where I am, whenever I see a sedge flying at dusk.

NOMENCLATURE

Throughout this book I have endeavoured to give both the common angling name as well as the scientific name for the sedges mentioned. A short time ago I read a review of a book, which mildly castigated the author for referring to the flies by their scientific name. The reviewer went on to say that in Britain we tend to use only the common name. I am afraid that this is so, but fly fishing, like entomology, is international. Confusion can occur if we only use the common name for a particular sedge as the same sedge may be called something else in Spain or in other parts of the world. If we refer to this insect by its correct scientific name, however, then there can be no confusion, for no matter what country you are in, a sedge such as the *Anabolia nervosa* is still going to be the *Anabolia nervosa*. It is time the British became less insular and accepted the fact that other countries have a legacy of fly fishing equal to our own.

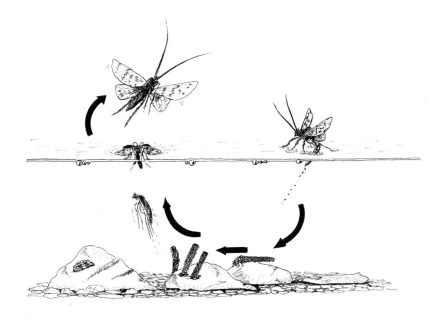

Life Cycle of the Sedge

CHAPTER ONE

THE NATURAL HISTORY OF THE SEDGE

Caddis in Amber

The sedges or caddis flies, as they are often termed, belong to the insect order Trichoptera (*trichos* appertaining to hair, and *ptera* meaning wing). They are also sometimes termed the roof-winged flies. The vast majority of them are aquatic flies, having a larval and pupal stage living in water. There are, however, a number of species of sedge fly whose habitat is wholly terrestrial. Worldwide there are in excess of 3,000 species, in the United Kingdom we have about 200, while the United States are blessed with approximately 1,200. The Trichoptera date back to the Carboniferous period of the world's history. Among the many inclusions found in Baltic amber, 147 species of sedge have been identified. All those years ago they had fluttered up into the pine trees only to be caught in the clinging resin and trapped in a fossil time warp. The interesting fact is that none of these ancient sedges are with us today; they are all extinct.

LIFE CYCLE

The sedges have what is termed a complete life cycle:

egg ... larva ... pupa ... adult.

This life cycle is similar to that of the Lepidoptera, the moths and butterflies. Other aquatic flies, such as the Ephemeroptera (mayflies), have no pupal stage and therefore have what is called by some entomologists an incomplete life cycle.

Eggs are laid in a number of different ways, depending on the species. In some, the females dip into the surface of the water to wash off the eggs. In others, the eggs are deposited on convenient vegetation, relying on rain or dew to wash them into the water. The females of a number of species oviposit by actually swimming beneath the surface, cocooned in a bubble of air, to lay their eggs on the river bottom. The eggs are protected from predation by a sticky gel which swells on contact with water.

From these eggs the larvae hatch out. Sedges hatch right throughout the fishing season, with large hatches occurring especially during late summer and early autumn. The larvae of many species construct for themselves protective cases made out of a wide variety of materials: sand, gravel, tiny pebbles and vegetable matter such as cut leaves or leaf stems. Others build no shelters but, with consummate skill, construct intricate nets or webs, similar to those spun by spiders. Some larvae are free swimming, while others rely on a safety strand of silk to anchor themselves to a convenient stone. When it is time to pupate, the case-making varieties seal up their larval shelters and pupate within, and even some of the non-case-making species construct a pupal shelter for this purpose. Within the safety of this case the larva changes into the pupa which already at this stage resembles the adult fly.

The pupae are equipped with special jaws which they use to break out of the confines of their pupal prison. The hatching pupa, or more precisely by now the hatching adult, climbs up some convenient water plant to reach the surface. Other species swim vigorously to the surface, using their intermediate long legs. Some are propelled by gases trapped within their outer protective skin.

Once at the surface the newly emerged adults either fly away or else run across the surface to the safety of dry land. This running action of the sedge is called 'skittering' by anglers. The adult flies are sombre-coloured creatures resembling dull-coloured moths, to which, of course, they are closely allied. They are related in as much as they have certain similarities in form, for example four wings, and in the evolutionary scale they may well have had a common ancestor. To put it another way, they are more akin to the Lepidoptera than shall we say to the mayflies, or beetles or true flies. Some moths look like sedges and many sedges resemble moths. A number of moth caterpillars construct shelters just like the caddis larvae, two examples being the aquatic moths, and the moths called *Psychidae*, known as bagworms from their habit of covering themselves with debris.

Throughout the world there are a number of wholly terrestrial caddis flies; one species, *Enoicyla pusilla*, is only found in the Forest of Wyre, in the English West Midlands. It creates a case of sand grains and usually feeds on dead leaves, oak in particular.

The sedge spends anything from a few days to a month or so as a winged adult. Its mouthparts are constructed for taking fluids: dew, rain droplets and in some instances nectar from flowering plants. The life cycle lasts a year; sometimes it is the eggs that overwinter but more often than not it is the larva that spends the winter months in the water.

Many species emerge at dusk and at night. Like moths they are attracted to light. Some of the larger species will travel quite long distances and are often taken in moth traps, situated some way from water. I have taken such sedges in my own moth trap, and I live at least half a mile from the nearest body of water. Fortunately for the fly fishermen, a number of sedges are diurnal, with a midday or early afternoon emergence, often prompting a rise from the trout and thus sport for the angler.

Sedges are to be found in all types of water: insignificant streamlets, wild moorland streams, sedate even-flowing chalk rivers. The smallest of ponds and the largest of lakes all harbour their share of the ubiquitous sedge family. In tropical parts of the world sedges are known to exist in small pools of water formed in the bowls of trees, and even in the water found in certain pitcher plants. The creatures found in such a micro-ecosystem form a study in themselves. Most species favour fairly shallow water, although some are to be found in the deepest parts of a lake or reservoir.

The scientific study of the Trichoptera is a comparatively recent thing, with serious work only commencing towards the second half of the last century. Entomologists from various parts of the world have contributed to our knowledge of this family of insects and observations by fly fishermen have made a useful contribution to this knowledge. Arguments and discussion still take place regarding various aspects of the life cycles of individual species and certainly concerning the classification of some others.

It is generally accepted that the Trichoptera are divided into two groups based on the larval forms, namely Campodeiform and Eruciform. The basic differences are shown in the illustrations. The two groups are further divided into eighteen families (some say twenty). In Great Britain we have thirteen families, as listed below.

BRITISH SEDGE FAMILIES

Campodeiform

CAMPODEIFORM

Rhyacophilidae
Polycentropidae

Hydroptilidae
Philopotamidae
Hydropsychidae
Psychomyiidae

Eruciform

ERUCIFORM

Limnephilidae
Phryganeidae
Sericostomatidae
Odontoceridae
Beraeidae
Leptoceridae
Molannidae

(The families not found on the British list are as follows: Plectro-tarsidae, Helicophidae, Philorheithidae, Philanisidae, Calam-oceratidae.)

We have looked briefly at the typical life cycle and also at the family classification, so now let us look in a little more detail at the adult insect. We have already stated that the flies themselves are sombre-coloured creatures, although one or two of them can be quite colourful when looked at closely. They have four wings and, unlike the moths and butterflies, whose wings are covered by colourful, minute scales, the sedge's wings are clothed in tiny hairs, hence the name Trichoptera.

The sedges are generally weak fliers and most shun the daylight hours, hiding up in the bankside vegetation until the sun has dipped below the skyline. It is then that they flutter from the reeds and bushes to dance in the air in nuptial flight. Mating usually takes place on convenient vegetation or on the ground, but a few will copulate on the wing. I have even witnessed such couplings take place on the actual water surface. As a general rule the male mounts the female then turns around so that he is facing the opposite direction. The female then seems to envelop the male with her wings. (The females are invariably larger than the males.) Eggs usually mature after a day or so.

CHAPTER TWO
THE CADDIS LARVA

In the Middle Ages, when roads were at best terrible and at worst non-existent, isolated village communities were served by bands of itinerant pedlars and hawkers. Apart from the goods they traded, they were also the bringers of news and often tellers of stories. One such pedlar was a purveyor of ribbons and braids as well as other inexpensive materials. In fact, he was a mobile walking haberdasher. In order to advertise both himself and his wares, he sewed bits of the braid and ribbons onto his apparel, so that the villagers and other potential customers could see straightaway who or what he was. Among the merchandise he sold was a cheap braid or yarn called caddis (in those days it could have been spelt in a number of different ways cadis, caddys, caddice). The industrious little worm that the people observed in the ponds and streams also bedecked itself with bits and pieces, so they christened it a 'caddis worm'. Now, whether this is true or not, I cannot say. It may, like the tales told by the ancient pedlars themselves, be just another story.

There is another school of thought that believes the root of the word caddis could possibly be derived from the same stem as 'caddy' as in teacaddy, being a box or case. I would like to believe the former derivation to be correct, if only for the fact that the story is a little more romantic.

Izaak Walton, in his *Compleat Angler*, refers to the creature in question as either a case-worm or caddis worm. It was also called a cod worm or cod bait. Even in those far-off days Walton realised the importance of the caddis larva as food for many kinds of fish. He also recognised a number of different species and noted how some occurred in some areas and not in others. He goes on to describe a number of individual and common species. Although we cannot correctly identify the larvae in question with any degree of certainty, we can make an educated guess.

The first caddis he mentions is 'The Piper', a caddis about 1 in long with a case made from a reed stem. He also mentions the fact that the bodies of the larvae change to a yellow colour when kept for a few days. This particular caddis is a little difficult to identify with any certain conviction, but one could hazard a guess and say it could well be a member of the Limnephilidae. This family includes the angler's sedge, the Cinnamon Sedge.

The second caddis Walton mentions as being a 'lesser caddis' and he calls this one the 'Cock-spur', made of husks, small gravel and slime and also sharp at one end. There is a strong possibility that this particular caddis could be a member of the family Leptoceridae. In this family we have the angler's flies, the Silverhorns and Grousewing. One member of this family, with a sharply curved case, is the species *Athripsodes aterrimus*, known by all fly fishermen as the Black Silverhorn.

The third sedge Walton describes as being not unlike a hedgehog. At least three Limnephilids come very close to this description – *L. rhombicus*, *L. flavicornis* and *L. politus*. All these caddis have cases with the materials arranged obliquely and I suppose that with a little imagination they could appear to look like small hedgehogs. Walton admits to not knowing what these caddis larvae turned into, but recognised the fact that there were many species for he states,

> I will tell you, scholar, several countries have several kinds of caddises, that differ as much as dogs do; that is to say, as much as a very cur and a greyhound do. These be bred in very little rills, or ditches, that run into bigger rivers; and I think a more proper bait for those rivers than any other.... I know not how, or of what, this caddis receives life, or what coloured fly it turns to; but doubtless they are the death of many trouts.

On the British list we have approximately 148 species that make a case of some sort; 28 form some sort of net or web; the rest are either free swimming or build some form of debris-covered silken tube.

CADDIS TYPES OF THE COMMON ANGLER'S SEDGE

THE CINNAMON SEDGE (*Limnephilus lunatus*)

The Eruciform larvae are found in both running and stillwater. The case is usually constructed from vegetable matter such as cut leaves, etc. Sometimes the case can be constructed from small discarded

L. lunatus

snail shells and also sand grains. The larva will use what is readily available. Length 20–23 mm, width 4 mm.

THE LARGE CINNAMON SEDGE (*Potamophylax latipennis*)

P. latipennis

The Eruciform larvae are found in both running and stillwater. The case is formed by small flat pebbles and large sand grains and is slightly curved. The size is approximately 20–22 mm. Other closely allied species could also be considered as Large Cinnamon Sedges, namely *P. cingulatus*, and also in Europe *P. rotundipennis*, both of whom construct similar cases with small stones and/or large sand grains.

THE BROWN SEDGE (*Anabolia nervosa*)

A. nervosa

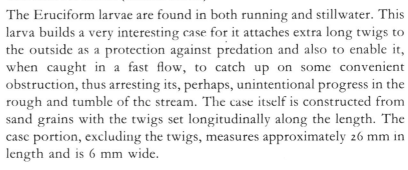

The Eruciform larvae are found in both running and stillwater. This larva builds a very interesting case for it attaches extra long twigs to the outside as a protection against predation and also to enable it, when caught in a fast flow, to catch up on some convenient obstruction, thus arresting its, perhaps, unintentional progress in the rough and tumble of the stream. The case itself is constructed from sand grains with the twigs set longitudinally along the length. The case portion, excluding the twigs, measures approximately 26 mm in length and is 6 mm wide.

THE MOTTLED SEDGE (*Glyphotaelius pellucidus*)

G. pellucidus

The Eruciform larvae are found in both running and stillwater. The case is unique, comprising pieces of leaves cut in almost true circles. Leaves of alder and hawthorn seem to be favoured. The case covers the larva which is extremely difficult to detect. It is difficult to give size details of this caddis case, but the actual larva measures approximately 23 mm.

THE GREAT RED SEDGE OR MURRAGH (*Phryganae grandis* OR *P. striata*)

P. grandis

The larval type of these species are termed sub-Eruciform. They are to be found in slow moving rivers and stillwater. The insects are quite large, as are the larvae, their cases measuring between 30 and 50 mm long and up to 9 mm wide. The cases are constructed from leaves and are spiralled, tapering slightly towards the rear. Other members of this family also construct similar cases; they are *P. obsoleta* and *P. varia*.

THE CAPERER (*Halesus radiatus* AND *H. digitatus*)

H. digitatus

The Eruciform larvae are found in both running and stillwater. The case is fabricated from a wide variety of materials – leaf debris, small stones, gravel, etc. On occasions it can resemble the larval cases of both *Limnephilus lunatus* and *Anabolia nervosa*, as small twigs are affixed longitudinally. The case can also be slightly curved in construction. It has a length of 23–27 mm and a width of about 4 mm.

H. radiatus

THE GRANNOM (*Brachycentrus subnubilus*)

The Eruciform larvae are found in streams and rivers. The case is constructed from vegetable matter and formed transversely into a rectangular shape. As the larva matures it continues to form the case from secretions only and the case becomes more circular. Length of the case is about 12 mm and the width 2–3 mm.

Brachycentrus subnubilus

THE SILVER OR GREY SEDGE (*Odontocerum albicorne*)

The Eruciform larvae are found in streams and rivers. The case is constructed from large smooth grains of sand and tapers towards the rear end. This end is blocked by a larger pebble, or pebbles, secured by a brown silk secretion. Length of the case is approximately 20 mm and it is 4 mm in width.

O. albicorne

THE BLACK SEDGE (*Athripsodes nigronervosus* OR *Silo nigricornis*)

Both larvae are Eruciform and both are found in rivers and in stillwater. According to Hickin in his book *Caddis Larvae*, there is no material available on the larval stage of this fly in Great Britain. However, McLachlan, in his work on European Trichoptera, advises that the case may be constructed from vegetable matter. The second species constructs a case from sand grains with small pebbles fixed along two sides; the length is about 8 mm and the width 4.5 mm.

THE SMALL SILVER SEDGE (*Lepidostoma hirtum*)

The Eruciform larvae are found in both still and running water. The case is formed from vegetable matter heavily cemented by the larva's secretions. It is square in shape and tapered towards the rear (not dissimilar to the case of the Grannom). In length the case is about 17–18 mm and is 2 mm wide.

L. hirtum

THE GROUSE WING (*Mystacides longicornis*)

The Eruciform larvae are found in rivers and stillwater, usually in large numbers. The case is constructed from grains of sand and is slightly curved and tapering towards the rear. In length it is approximately 15 mm with a width of 1.5 mm.

M. longicornis

M. azurea

M. nigra

A. aterrimus

A. cinereus

S. personatum

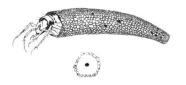

T. waeneri

Rhyacophila sp

THE BLACK SILVERHORN (*Mystacides azurea*, *M. nigra* OR *Athripsodes aterrimus*)

The Eruciform larvae are found in all types of water from small streams to large reservoirs. The case of *M. nigra* is constructed from grains of sand with occasional bits of vegetable matter adhering. The case of *M. azurea* is composed of both vegetable fragments and small stones, with a few twigs stuck on the sides longitudinally. The third larva, *A. aterrimus*, has a case constructed from grains of sand. The case is curved and strongly tapered to the rear. The length of the cases of the first two is the same at 15 mm, with a width of 1.5 mm. The case of the third larva is larger, at 18 mm and 2 mm in width.

THE BROWN SILVERHORN (*Athripsodes cinereus* OR *A. albifrons*)

The Eruciform larvae are found in all types of water. Both construct cases of sand grains. The cases are tapered. In length the cases are approximately 12 mm with a width of 2 mm. The adult *A. Albifrons* is distinguished from the normal Brown Silverhorn by two small white triangles on the anterior wing.

THE WELSHMAN'S BUTTON (*Sericostoma personatum*)

The Eruciform larvae are found in streams, rivers and stillwater. The case is made from largish sand grains and slightly curved. The rear end is sealed by a secretion and has a central hole. The case is about 15 mm long and 3 mm wide.

THE SMALL RED SEDGE (*Tinodes waeneri*)

A number of other species could well fill the appellation 'Red Sedge', but *T. waeneri* is a Campodeiform non-case-making larva which fabricates a silken tube onto which are stuck sand grains, vegetable matter and algaeic matter. The tube is grey. The length of the tube is about 30–35 mm and it is up to 2 mm wide.

THE SAND FLY (*Rhyacophila dorsalis*)

This is a Campodeiform larva and is usually a river species. It builds no case as a larva but constructs a shelter from gravel when it is time to pupate. The larva is entirely free living. The length of the larva is approximately 22–25 mm. It is usually a greeny colour.

THE GREY FLAG (*Hydropsyche instabilis*, *H. pellucidula* OR *H. angustipennis*)

The Campodeiform larvae are found in rivers. Non-case-making, they build a rough shelter and spin a funnel-like web. The exposed portions of the web gather debris of all sorts. The current sweeps various prey into the web and into the waiting jaws of the predatory larva. In size it is approximately 17 mm long.

THE MARBLED SEDGE (*Hydropsyche contubernalis*)

Hydropsyche sp

This is a Campodeiform larva and, like the other *Hydropsyche* species, this one is a river species. It probably constructs a similar web to the other larvae in the family.

THE SMALL YELLOW SEDGE (*Psychomyia pusilla*)

The Campodeiform larvae are found in all types of running water. Non-case-making, the larva constructs a silk tube underneath stones, etc. The larva is about 8 mm long with a width of approximately 1.5 mm.

THE LONGHORNS (*Oecetis lacustris* OR *O. ochracea*)

The Eruciform larvae are found in ponds and lakes. The case is constructed from fine grains of sand and is heavily tapered towards the rear end. The case length is approximately 8–10 mm with a breadth of 1.4–1.6 mm *O. ochracea* constructs a case of larger sand grains and vegetable matter. It is slightly curved. The length is approximately 16 mm, and the breadth about 3 mm.

THE MEDIUM SEDGE (*Goera pilosa*)

G. pilosa

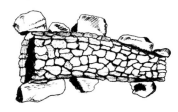

The Eruciform larvae are found in all types of water. The case is constructed from sand and gravel with larger pieces of gravel or small stones stuck to the outside. The sand portion of the case is slightly curved and flattened on the underside. In size the case is 15 mm long and 4.5 mm wide. The addition of the small stones extends the width to about 10 mm.

THE DARK SEDGE (*Polycentropus flavomaculatus*)

Campodeiform larva. This species is reckoned to be one of the most abundant of sedges. It is found mainly in running water of all types and can also be found in the margins of some lakes which are subjected to wind and wave motion. The larva constructs a small purse-like net underneath convenient stones (Hickin likens them to miniature swallows' nests). The length of the larva is approximately 12–14 mm.

BICOLOR SEDGE (*Triaenodes bicolor*)

This Eruciform larva is a still-water species. The larva is an active creature, swimming by means of its long hairy middle legs. It

T. bicolor

constructs its case out of regularly shaped leaves. The case is spiralled along its length and strongly tapered, looking very much like the tip of a water reed. In length it is about 35 mm and in breadth 2.0–2.5 mm.

THE YELLOW SPOTTED SEDGE (*Diplectrona felix*)

This Campodeiform larva, a member of the Hydropsychidae family, favours fast moving small streams and rivers. Like its allied species it lives under stones and probably utilises similar funnel-type webs. The insect is a little smaller than the other species so one can assume that the larva will be also.

THE DARK SPOTTED SEDGE (*Philopotamus montanus*)

A Campodeiform larva, this caddis likes fast moving water and constructs a purse-like net beneath stones, etc. The size of the larva is approximately 22 mm long.

I have included the last three species for purely personal reasons. I mention the Triaenodes because it is a widely distributed species. I have found it on a number of day-ticket reservoirs in the south of England and it is also common in Europe. I felt it worth including because, as the larva is free swimming, it is likely to receive the trout's attention. Autopsies on the stomach contents of caught fish tend to prove this.

The second sedge I have called the Yellow Spotted Sedge because of its wing markings. I have caught this particular fly on a number of mountain streams in North Wales, though it is best described as being local in distribution. The last sedge, *P. montanus*, I have taken in quite large numbers on the rivers in Devon and North Wales and, furthermore, it is a common sedge in France and Spain, where a number of imitations of the adult are to be found.

The rest of the insects given are sedges of proven fly-fishing lineage, most of them recognised by trout anglers everywhere. In Europe, where the members of the order Trichoptera are far more numerous than in Britain, the British nomenclature still seems to apply even though the actual insect may well be a closely related species and not the specific fly given in the British list. The same thing can occur in certain areas of the UK; a sedge that is local and prolific on a specific river or lake can well take on the mantle of, shall we say, the Brown Sedge or the Red Sedge, even though the actual insects are not the ones quoted above.

Before concluding this chapter, mention should be made of the diet of the caddis larva. Many are omnivorous; a good number are purely herbivorous browsers, some are active predators and not averse to feeding upon the smaller members of their own family. As a rough guide most of the web- and net-makers are carnivorous and, as a generalisation, the opposite holds for the case-makers.

CHAPTER THREE
THE MICROCADDIS

Micro Sedge Tiny Grey
Agapetus sp

All the larvae and their subsequent winged adults mentioned in the last chapter are of a size that can be easily seen and noted by the angler. However, a large number of sedges that are food for trout can, by their very size, remain unnoticed by most fishermen. The importance of the microcaddis, as they are termed, is a comparatively recent appreciation. Due entirely to their size, they have been inadvertently ignored by most anglers. At both larval and final winged stages they are only 5 mm to a very maximum of 8 mm in length, so it seems reasonable that such small creatures have been missed by many anglers. On the other hand, equally minute creatures, such as small midges and reed smuts, as well as other fauna both terrestrial and aquatic, have been used for some considerable time by both river and still-water fishermen. Take, for example, the tiny aquatic mites sometimes found in the stomach contents of trout. Flies have been devised to imitate such creatures, so why not the tiny sedges?

In the UK there is a decided lack of established patterns for such sedges. I tend to adapt existing flies and scale these down in size, tying up various coloured sedges on tiny hooks around size 18 to size 20. In recent years, on the various rivers that I have fished, I have found that my success rate has gone up considerably since I resorted to using small flies for general dry fly fishing. Nowadays any hook above size 14 looks extremely large to me and I very rarely fish anything larger now on some of the wild rivers. The micro sedges come from a number of different sedge families, two of which are described below. In this chapter I shall only give the larval form and description and shall describe the adults later. The common names given to the flies are my own. As a general rule most of these minute sedges are of a greyish-brown colour, mainly due to the pubescent hairs on the wing.

THE MICRO SEDGE TINY GREY (*Agapetus fuscipes*)

The Eruciform larvae are found in swift flowing rivers and streams. The case is constructed from small irregular stones. It is curved at the top and flattened on the bottom. This type of case is described by American anglers as a 'saddle case'. Very large numbers of this sedge can occur on some streams. The larva is about 5 mm long.

A. fuscipes

THE MICRO SEDGE TINY BLACK (*Hydroptila sparsa*)

The Campodeiform larvae are found mostly in streams. The case is constructed from very fine sand grains. The dorsal surface is convex and the ventral surface flat. The size is approximately 4–5 mm.

H. sparsa

There are many other species of sedge which are small and yet very abundant. In some areas they can be the most prolific sedge. One caddis larva of the species *Orthotrichia* constructs a silken case not unlike a flask or milk bottle in shape.

Oxyethira sp

CHAPTER FOUR

THE ADULT SEDGE

It would be extremely convenient to be able to tell at a glance what species of sedge is on the water. It is true to say that the practised eye of an experienced fisherman can generally do this, but correct identification of the family of sedges is no easy matter. Many species vary so little in size and colour that identification is only possible by means of a microscope. Expert classification usually entails very close examination of various aspects of the sedge's anatomy. Differences in parts of the head, sometimes in the configuration of the legs and antennae and certainly of the genitalia, are the only means by which correct identification can be made. It is always a dangerous thing to identify solely by colour, for the minute hairs on the wing can often be rubbed off, especially with the Grouse Wing Sedge. The lighter barring on the wings can thus disappear, causing the fly to look more like a Brown Silverhorn. In some flies there is too wide a variance in both size and colour within the same species for positive identification to be made just by casual observation.

The following list should be considered as a rough and ready guide for the angler and not a formal entomological key to species identification. Sufficient information is given to enable the fly fisherman to recognise the probable difference in species, allowing him or her to match the hatch with the contents of the fly box. This list, combined with the list indicating the emergence times of the adult flies, allows the angler at least to hazard an intelligent guess as to the species. I have also endeavoured to indicate geographical distribution as an additional aid to identification.

SEDGE RECOGNITION

THE CINNAMON SEDGE (*Limnephilus lunatus*)

This is one of the most popular of the sedges used by fly fishermen. A number of different flies are tied to represent it. The colour of the anterior wings, as its name suggests, is a cinnamon-brown marked with various patches of darker brown and black. A half-moon shape situated at the posterior end of the wing distinguishes this species of *Limnephilus* and gives it the name *lunatus*. The body varies in colour but generally it is greenish.

L. lunatus

Size of wings: males 13–14 mm; females 14–15 mm. The antennae can best be described as medium in length.

The species is widely distributed throughout Great Britain and Europe and is found in all of the fly-fishing countries of Europe including France, Spain, Austria, Germany, Italy and Yugoslavia. This sedge does not hatch out in large numbers like some of the other sedges, but it is prolific enough to be a very important angler's fly.

THE LARGE CINNAMON SEDGE (*Potamophylax latipennis*)

P. latipennis

This is just one of a number of larger Limnephilids that can be described as a Large Cinnamon Sedge. Other such species include *P. rotundapennis*, *Limnephilus rhombicus*, *L. flavicornis* and *L. marmoratus*. In the species *P. latipennis* the colour of the wings can best be described as a mousey-brown with a number of pale patches. The shape of the anterior wings is very much more rounded than in *L. lunatus* and, of course, a little larger.

Size of wings: male 18 mm; female 18–19 mm.

The fly is a widely distributed species found in most parts of Europe. It can be seen flying at dusk along the rivers, often in quite large numbers. Where and when this sedge occurs makes this fly an important one for the fly fisherman.

THE BROWN SEDGE (*Anabolia nervosa*)

A. nervosa

This fly, which sounds very much like a wasting disease, is, as its name suggests, of an overall light brown shade. Even the antennae, which are of medium length, are brown. The body is blackish above and reddish-brown beneath. The wings are a dull brown with the same tinge of red. The wings also have two pale spots or patches.

Size of wing: male 11–14 mm; female 12–16 mm.

It can be found on some rivers in very large numbers. Mosley, in his major work on *British Caddis Flies*, states that this species varies greatly in both size and colour. Very abundant in Western Europe.

THE MOTTLED SEDGE (*Glyphotaelius pellucidus*)

This is one of the more attractive sedges and quite easily recognised at a glance. The posterior of the anterior wings is distinctively

G. pellucidus

scalloped. The colour of the wings is a yellowish-grey, heavily mottled with dark brown and black, hence its common name. This mottling is extremely variable and as a general rule the males are more heavily marked than the females. The body is generally of a dull green.

Wing length: male and female 17 mm.

This species is both common and widespread in Europe. It is the only species in this family to be found in Great Britain. It is one of the species I have identified on my local fishing water in Kent.

THE GREAT RED SEDGE OR MURRAGH (*Phryganae grandis* OR *P. striata*)

P. grandis

P. striata

One of the best known of the angler's sedges, it is often referred to by its Irish name 'the Murragh'. For the purpose of fishing there is nothing to choose between either of these two large sedge flies. *P. grandis* can be identified by a continuous black line running across the anterior wing. In *P. striata* the line is broken and the markings patchier. The overall colour of the wings is also slightly different. McLachlan describes the wings of *P. grandis* as being cinereous, and those of *P. striata* as browner. The body of the former is described as being fuscous and the latter as being a shade darker.

Wing size: *P. grandis* approximately 20 mm in the male; 27 mm in the female. *P. striata* 23 mm in the male; 26 mm in the female.

Both species are very well distributed throughout Europe, including all of the major fly-fishing countries.

THE SPECKLED PETER (*Phryganae varia*)

P. varia

As its name indicates, this fly has heavily speckled wings – far more heavily marked than *P. grandis* or *P. striata*. The wings are more elongated and of a dark grey colour marked with black. There are also three distinguishing white spots on the wing. The body is almost black in colour with the segmentation of an ochre shade. This sedge is also considerably smaller than the other two given.

Size of wing: male 15 mm; female 17 mm.

Like the other two sedges in the family it is widely distributed in Europe, although McLachlan states that it had not been found in either Spain or Italy at the time when he compiled his treatise (1874–80). It may well be included in the Spanish and Italian checklists by now, but I have no further information on this.

P. obsoleta

THE PETER OR DARK PETER (*Phryganae obsoleta*)

A closely allied species to the last sedge but again a little smaller and darker. A smaller than usual posterior wing identifies this species.

The body is black with grey segmentations and the wings are also a dark brownish-grey with black reticulations. The wing is somewhat broader than in *P. varia*.

Wing size: male 12 mm; female 15 mm.

This fly is reckoned to be a northern species and from mountainous areas. Both the Peters are popular flies in Ireland.

THE CAPERER (*Halesus radiatus* AND *H. digitatus*)

H. radiatus

A large sedge popular with anglers. The colour of the anterior wings is a light yellowy-brown with grey-bordered cross veins. There are also some heavy dark grey streaks, giving a striated effect to the wing. The anterior wings are very broad. The body is a greyish-brown and the legs are yellow with black hairs. The body of *H. digitatus* is somewhat darker than *H. radiatus* and the overall size of the fly is a little larger.

Wing sizes: *H. radiatus*, male and female 20 mm; *H. digitatus* male and female 23 mm.

The two species are common in the British Isles and in many European countries including Yugoslavia, Austria and as far south as northern Greece.

THE GRANNOM (*Brachycentrus subnubilus*)

B. subnubilus

This sedge is sometimes called the Greentail by fly fishermen because the female displays her eggs at the tip of her abdomen and these eggs become very noticeably green as they mature. This sedge can often hatch out in very large numbers, especially on the southern chalk streams of England, which can prompt a selective feeding response from the trout. The Grannom is not a very large sedge. Its wings are a smoky-grey covered by a yellow pubescence in such a way as to give an impression of small yellow spots and patches. The body is generally black in colour.

Size of wing: male 9 mm; female 11 mm.

This sedge is distributed right through Europe, including the USSR.

THE SILVER OR GREY SEDGE (*Odontocerum albicorne*)

O. albicorne

This is quite a large sedge of an overall silvery-grey appearance. I have seen large numbers hatching on the River Itchen in Hampshire in September and have also witnessed trout feeding avidly upon them in June on the River Krka in Slovenia. The body of the sedge is black, covered with grey hairs. The anterior wings are grey and densely covered by a silvery-grey pubescence; older sedges tend to turn a little yellow.

Size of wing: male 13 mm; female 18 mm.

This sedge is found in most of the fly-fishing countries of Europe.

S. nigricornis

THE BLACK SEDGE (*Athripsodes nigronervosus* OR *Silo nigricornis*)

These two contenders for the name Black Sedge come from different sedge families, the former belonging to the Leptoceridae and the latter to the family Sericostomatidae. Let us look at the species *A. nigronervosus* first. The body is black, as are the wings which are heavily neurated.

Size of wing: male 13 mm; female 11 mm.

A. nigronervosus

This sedge is a very strong flyer and is found on both stillwater and large rivers throughout Central and Northern Europe.

The other sedge, *Silo nigricornis*, is another black sedge, but only the males of the species are black; the females are brown so we will ignore the female and describe only the male. The body is dark, almost black, the wings are dark grey to black and the posterior wing has an angled groove running down its length. This is an identification feature.

Wing length: male 9 mm; female 10 mm.

The species is widely distributed from Sweden right down to Slovenia and in most areas of Great Britain.

L. hirtum

THE SMALL SILVER SEDGE (*Lepidostoma hirtum*)

This is one of Europe's most common sedges. The body is a pale grey and the wings are a smoky-grey sprinkled with blackish scales. The female is a shade lighter in the wing, with slightly yellow pubescent hair. The female, like the Grannom female, shows a green egg mass at the tip of the abdomen.

Wing size; male and female 9 mm.

This particular sedge has been noted as far north as Lapland and also right down into Southern Europe.

M. longicornis

THE GROUSE WING (*Mystacides longicornis*)

The anterior wings of this sedge look for all the world like two slips of feather taken from the wing of a grouse. The body of the insect is brown with pale lateral lines. The antennae are long and whitish in colour. The posterior wing is smoky-grey and fringed with white hairs. The anterior wings are golden strongly marked with dark patches or bands; in some specimens these black markings are absent.

Length of wing; male 9 mm; female 8 mm.

It is a very abundant sedge on stillwater, although I have also seen this insect on the slower parts of some rivers.

THE BLACK SILVERHORN (*Mystacides azurea* OR *M. Nigra*)

M. azurea

The most notable characteristic of *M. nigra* is its long, heavily banded antennae. In the species *M. azurea* the antennae tend to be lighter and have fewer markings. The eyes of *M. nigra* are a distinct red, while the eyes of *M. azurea* are brown. The wings of *M. azurea* have a bluish metallic cast, while those of *M. nigra* are somewhat duller. The bodies of both of them are the same, namely a dark brownish-grey.

M. nigra

The size of wings are the same in both species: male 9 mm; female 8 mm.

Both species are found on all types of water, running and still. They occur all over Europe. Another sedge, also called the Black Silverhorn, is the species *Athripsodes aterrimus*. This is a long-antennaed insect with a black body and, generally, black wings. McLachlan mentions a variety of this sedge with brown, not black, wings.

Wing size: male 9 mm; female 8 mm.

McLachlan maintained that the black variety is predominant in the northern part of Europe, while the brown variety is more common in southern countries.

THE BROWN SILVERHORN (*Athripsodes cinereus* OR *A. albifrons*)

A. cinereus

A. cinereus has been described as very variable when it comes to physical markings. The body of the male is a dark brownish-grey, while that of the female can show a greenish cast. The antennae are long and each segment has a white banding on its lower portion. The wings are generally brown but, as stated, they can vary considerably.

Size of wings: male 10 mm; female 8 mm.

A. albifrons

A. albifrons tends to be very similar to *cinereus*, but with distinct white triangles and slashes of white on the anterior wing. I have found specimens of this sedge on the River Exe in Devon.

Both species are widely distributed all over Europe, *A. albifrons* being more local in occurrence.

THE WELSHMAN'S BUTTON (*Sericostoma personatum*)

S. personatum

It is difficult to understand why Halford or Lunn should have so named this sedge, for the name Welshman's Button refers to a small beetle of the Celtic fringes, *Phylopertha horticola*, the June Bug, Field Chafer or Coch y Bonddu. If it was not Halford or Lunn, then it must be someone else who got it all wrong. It is also something of an enigma as to why one artificial was given a bright yellow band in the middle of the body. The body of the fly is dark brown, sometimes with a greenish cast. The anterior wings can be described as a darkish chestnut-brown and clothed with golden hairs. A whitish patch can be seen on the top edge of the wing when the wings are closed.

Wing size: male 12 mm; female 15 mm.

A common European species.

T. waeneri

THE SMALL RED SEDGE (*Tinodes waeneri*)

A number of other species could be classified as Red Sedge; the species *T. aureola* and *T. assimilis* are but two that are closely allied to *T. waeneri*. In fact, *T. assimilis* is a species local to my area in Kent. The wings of all the species mentioned are grey clothed in golden grey hair, giving the fly an overall reddish coloration. The body is yellowish-red and the antennae are short and stout.

All three species occur in most European countries.

Wing size: male and female 6–8 mm.

R. dorsalis

THE SAND FLY (*Rhyacophila dorsalis*)

This fly is sometimes known as Ronalds's Sand Fly after the eminent nineteenth-century angling entomologist Alfred Ronalds. The body is a brownish grey; the wings can best be termed as greyish-yellow with darker markings; there is a blotch on the top of the wing, which is seen when the insect is viewed from above with the wings folded at rest.

The size of wings is variable. In fact, Mosley, in his book *British Trichoptera*, does not give a size, but judging from the specimens I have taken in the past I would say the wing varies from 12–15 mm. John Goddard suggests they can be as small as 10 mm and as large as 15 mm.

There is widespread distribution throughout Great Britain and Europe including the fishing areas of Spain. A closely allied species is found in the sub-Alpine and Alpine districts of Europe. This is *R. obliterata*, which has much yellower wings.

H. instabilis

THE GREY FLAG (*Hydropsyche instabilis, H. pellucidula* OR *H. angustipennis*)

The term 'flag' is a generic term for sedges in Ireland. *H. instabilis* is considered to be a localised sedge occurring on rocky rivers usually at altitude. The body is slightly greenish. The wings are pale yellowy-white, finely reticulated with brownish-grey and pale patches, giving the impression of being spotted. All three insects are very similar in appearance.

Size of wing: male 11 mm; female 12 mm.

Examples of the family Hydropsyche are common right through Europe. The Grey Flag is one of the most predominant species of sedge found on my local river in Kent, the River Darent.

THE MARBLED SEDGE (*Hydropsyche contubernalis*)

H. contubernalis

This sedge was previously called *H. ornatula*, and there is another closely allied species, which is very similar in colour and markings, called *H. guttata*. The body of the Marbled Sedge is of a greenish hue. The wings are a brownish-grey but heavily marked and spotted in white, giving a marbled effect.

Size of wing: male 11 mm; female 12 mm.

This sedge can be considered local in certain areas, but is also well distributed throughout Europe.

THE SMALL YELLOW SEDGE (*Psychomyia pusilla*)

P. pusilla

One of the smaller angler's sedges. The body is a reddish-brown and its legs are yellow. The anterior wings are covered in a dense yellow pubescence and fringed with yellowish-grey.

Size of wings: male 5 mm; female 6 mm.

These flies can be found in very large numbers, for they hatch out in thousands. Widely distributed in the British Isles and through most of Europe.

THE LONGHORNS (*Oecetis lacustris* OR *O. ochracea*)

O. lacustris

The Longhorn sedges are considered to be important flies on some British reservoirs. The body of the fly is greenish in colour. The antennae are long (hence its angling name) and of a greyish-ochre colour. The wings are somewhat glassy and densely covered with a greyish-brown pubescence, lightly marked in darker grey.

Size of wing: male 7 mm; female 8 mm.

The species *Oecetis ochracea* is a slightly larger fly with a yellowish tinge on the wings.

Size: male 13 mm; female 11 mm.

Both species are universal on stillwater throughout Europe.

BICOLOR SEDGE (*Triaenodes bicolor*)

T. bicolor

I have found this sedge on a number of day-ticket reservoirs in the south of England and consider it worthy of inclusion. The body is brown, the antennae are a yellowish-white and annulated with black. The anterior wings are narrow and clothed in a reddish pubescence, while the posterior wings contrast by being black and grey-fringed. An easily recognised sedge, it is found near weedy water and is well distributed. Size of wing: male 7–8 mm; female 10 mm.

D. felix

THE YELLOW SPOTTED SEDGE (*Diplectrona felix*)

The body is brown as are the antennae. The anterior wings are brown, covered by yellow spots.

Size of wing: male 7 mm; female 9 mm.

This species is considered to be extremely local in its habitat, favouring streams that run through woods. In his latest book, *Waterside Guide*, John Goddard has also included a Yellow Spotted Sedge, the species *Cyrnus trimaculatus*. This fly is similar to the Dark Sedge *Polycentropus flavomaculatus* given below. It has also been identified in France.

G. pilosa

THE MEDIUM SEDGE (*Goera pilosa*)

A robust medium-sized sedge with an overall hairy appearance. There is only one British species in this family. The sedge has an overall greyish-yellow appearance. The anterior wings are clothed in a yellowish-grey pubescence and have a small irregular patch of wing with no hairs on it at all. This can be used as a recognition factor in helping to identify the species.

This is a common species, found in most countries.

Size of wing: male 10 mm; female 12 mm.

P. flavomaculatus

THE DARK SEDGE (*Polycentropus flavomaculatus*)

John Bickerdyke, in his book *The Book of the All Round Angler*, mentions three dark sedges, namely the one mentioned above, *Drusus annulatus* and *Chaetoptryx villosa*. The most widely distributed is the dark sedge *P. flavomaculatus*. The antennae of this sedge are dark brown. The wings are also a dark brownish-grey with a pubescence of variable yellow spots.

Size of wings: male 7 mm; female 9 mm.

It is common throughout Europe from Corsica in the south right up to Lapland. David Jacques, in his survey of Two Lakes in Hampshire, includes it as one of the identified species from that water.

P. montanus

THE DARK SPOTTED SEDGE (*Philopotamus montanus*)

This is a very common sedge and is often imitated by fly fishermen. I have called it The Dark Spotted to differentiate between it and the other spotted sedge, the Yellow Spotted. It is one pattern that is used in France. I have witnessed a number of good daytime hatches on the rivers in Devon and North Wales. The body is very dark and clothed with yellow hairs. The anterior wing is also dark and spotted with irregular yellow spots. The posterior wing is also lightly spotted.

Wing sizes: both male and female 11 mm.

This species is usually found at altitude on fast moving streams.

THE MICRO SEDGE TINY GREY (*Agapetus fuscipes*)

A. fuscipes

This is a very common and widely distributed species, its anterior wings are a dark smokey-grey, covered with a reddish-grey pubescence.

The size of the wing is approximately the same in both the sexes, 5 mm.

It is common in France, Switzerland and Germany as well as all over the British Isles.

THE MICRO SEDGE TINY BLACK (*Hydroptila sparsa*)

H. sparsa

The body of this small sedge has a greenish tinge. The anterior wings are black or very dark grey and covered with raised deep-black hairs. The wings are much slimmer than in many other sedges.

The anterior wing measures about the same in the male and female, 3 mm. The sedge is found in running water and is a common species in Northern and Central Europe. These small sedges can offer be seen running over the stones that fringe the river. In fact, on my local water they are even to be found in the anglers' boats.

EMERGENCE TIMES

The following list of sedge emergence times (or when the sedge is actually on the wing), concerns the British Isles, although in many instances the same times will apply to other parts of Europe. Temperature and general weather conditions can, of course, affect such emergence, so it is highly likely that the further south one goes the earlier the sedges could appear and, conversely, the further north one goes, the later the sedges will make their appearance. In southern Alpine areas where rivers can be affected by such things as snow melt, it is possible that the sedges may tend to emerge at a later time, so one can only give a rough guide. To put it another way, I would not set my watch by them, nature will always do things in her own sweet time.

From time to time one will see sedges emerging, or at least on the wing, in months other than those listed above. I have seen the Dark Spotted Sedge, for instance, as early as April and as late as

	APRIL	MAY	JUNE	JULY	AUGUST	SEPT.	OCT.
The Bicolor Sedge			×	×	×	×	
The Black Sedge			×				
The Black Silverhorn		×	×	×	×	×	
The Brown Sedge				×		×	×
The Brown Silverhorn		×	×	×	×		
The Caperer					×	×	×
The Cinnamon Sedge		×	×	×	×	×	×
The Dark Peter				×	×	×	×
The Dark Sedge		×	×	×	×	×	
The Dark Spotted Sedge	×	×	×	×	×		
The Grannom	×	×					
The Great Red Sedge		×	×	×			
The Grey Flag	×	×	×	×	×	×	×
The Grouse Wing		×	×	×	×	×	
The Large Cinnamon Sedge				×	×	×	
The Longhorns		×	×	×	×	×	
The Marbled Sedge	×	×	×	×	×	×	×
The Medium Sedge		×	×	×	×		
The Micro Sedge Tiny Black		×			×	×	
The Micro Sedge Tiny Grey		×	×	×	×	×	×
The Mottled Sedge		×	×	×	×	×	×
The Sand Fly	×	×	×	×	×	×	×
The Silver Sedge			×	×	×	×	×
The Small Red Sedge		×	×	×	×	×	×
The Small Silver Sedge	×		×	×	×	×	
The Small Yellow	×	×	×	×	×	×	×
The Speckled Peter				×	×	×	×
The Welshman's Button			×	×	×		
The Yellow Spotted Sedge			×	×	×		

September. The secret is not to be surprised at what nature dishes up for us at the waterside. Long hard winters, mild winters, cold spring conditions, a late spring – in fact any extreme in the weather can affect the emergence of any aquatic insect, accelerating or slowing up their appearance on the water. For the fisherman, the time of day when he is likely to see sedges on the wing is also of importance. It is fortunate that not all species hatch out during the hours of darkness, when all good fishermen should be tucked up in bed. Many sedges choose to emerge during daylight hours, coinciding with the angler's visit to the lake or stream.

TIME OF DAY

The Bicolor Sedge	daytime and evening
The Black Sedge	late afternoon/dusk
The Black Silverhorn	daytime and evening
The Brown Sedge	evening
The Brown Silverhorn	daytime and evening
The Caperer	late afternoon/dusk
The Cinnamon Sedge	daytime and evening
The Dark Peter	evening
The Dark Sedge	daytime and evening

The Dark Spotted Sedge	daytime
The Grannom	daytime and evening
The Great Red Sedge	evening
The Grey Flag	daytime
The Grouse Wing	daytime and evening
The Large Cinnamon Sedge	late afternoon/dusk
The Longhorns	daytime and evening
The Marbled Sedge	late afternoon/dusk
The Medium Sedge	daytime and evening
The Micro Sedge Tiny Black	evening
The Micro Sedge Tiny Grey	evening
The Mottled Sedge	daytime and evening
The Sand Fly	daytime
The Silver Sedge	daytime and evening
The Small Silver Sedge	evening
The Small Red Sedge	evening
The Small Yellow Sedge	evening
The Speckled Peter	evening
The Welshman's Button	daytime and evening
The Yellow Spotted Sedge	daytime and evening

During the daytime many of the sedges which emerge or fly in the evening may also be found on the water for the purpose of egg laying. On more than one occasion I have had fine sport with the dry sedge in mid-morning. Two occasions stand out in my mind. One was on a stretch of the River Torridge in Devon. The trout on that day were concerned with taking two species of insects. The first was the golden yellow stonefly, the Yellow Sally, the females of which species were returning to the water to lay their eggs. They were fluttering above the surface of the river like so many pieces of breeze-blown yellow confetti.

The second insect was a medium-sized sedge. These were flying above the river and every so often they descended to wash off the eggs on the tips of their abdomens. The trout were taking both insects with relish – a main meal complete with caviar!

The other time occurred quite recently. I was lucky enough to be on one of the fine Slovenian chalk streams, the Krka. This river is famed for its evening rise to the sedge, but on the few days I was there all the activity occurred in the morning with egg-laying adults and in the afternoon with emerging sedges. In their anxiety to get at the ovipositing sedges, the trout were leaping right out of the water and diving down on top of the flies as they dipped the surface.

As a fly fisherman one should always remember to expect the unexpected. A sedge can be found on the water at any time of the day (or night). This applies both to rivers and still water. Trout seldom, if ever, ignore a sedge on the surface and, as anglers, we should endeavour to keep our eyes open for the first sign of sedge activity.

CHAPTER FIVE
CADDIS LARVAE IMITATIONS

There is no doubt that trout feed at times on caddis larvae, but the true importance of the larval stage in the diet of the trout is open to question. I suppose if it is hungry enough a trout will, as a matter of course, eat practically anything that moves within its domain. I have often taken trout crammed with caddis cases, and I have caught trout when I have been using imitations devised with a cased caddis in mind. There is a school of thought that flies tied to imitate such encased larvae are a bit of a waste of time and that a trout will only be tempted to take the fly out of some form of desperation. The hypothesis put forward is that a trout would prefer to feed on something soft and succulent like an uncased larva. This may well be true, but if the predominant species in the ecology of that particular water was a caddis encased in sand or vegetable matter, and this creature was crawling along the bottom, would the trout ignore it? I think not. In fact, if a species were in such numbers as can occur with caddis, then the trout could possibly feed on them almost to the exclusion of anything else, cases included. When you think about it, our quarry is not averse to taking such hard-backed creatures as crayfish, and what about snails? So why not the humble caddis?

THE ARTIFICIAL

The following caddis imitations are taken from both sides of the Atlantic as well as from Europe. Both case- and non-case-making larvae are imitated by modern and traditional patterns.

THE STICK FLY

This fly can best be described as a broad-spectrum pattern. It can be used to imitate a number of aquatic creatures – a hatching

Chironomid midge, a damsel larva and, of course, a cased caddis of sorts. It can be fished at all levels. If one is using it as a hatching buzzer (Chironomid) then it is at its most successful fished close to the surface. If, on the other hand, it is a caddis larva we have in mind, then it is fished well below the surface and usually close to the bottom. This is a very easy fly to tie. I have always been a believer in the theory that the simpler the pattern, the more effective it can be.

Step by step: Stick Fly

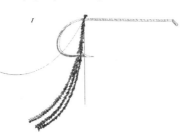

DRESSING

Hook	Mustad 38941 or 79580 long shank sizes 8–14
Thread	Black pre-waxed
Tail	None
Body	Bronze peacock herl
Rib	(Optional) fine gold or copper wire
Thorax	Fluorescent green or yellow floss
Hackle	Brown partridge or natural red cock or hen hackle

METHOD

Step 1   Wind the thread down the shank and there tie in about three strands of peacock herl and a length of fine copper wire.

Step 2   Return the silk about four–fifths of the way back down the shank and follow this with the peacock herl. It is best if you twist it into a rope first.

Step 3   Wind on the wire rib in the opposite way to the herl (this prevents the ribbing falling into the turns of the herl.) After removing any excess herl and ribbing wire and tying off, tie in a length of fluorescent silk.

Step 4   Now wind on the silk portion of the body and tie off and cut away any excess silk. Tie in a few turns of hackle to imitate the legs. Form a neat head, whip finish and finish with a drop of clear varnish.

THE GREEN STICK

This fly is devised to imitate the swimming cased larva of the sedge *Triaenodes bicolor*, the Bicolor Sedge. I have come across this caddis on a number of waters in the South of England and have no doubt that it appears on many other still waters. It is most likely to be encountered in marginal areas where a healthy weed growth occurs, for it swims around such weed beds. It goes without saying, therefore, that this is where one would fish the artificial. Like the previous fly, this is also a very simple fly to construct.

Step by step: Green Stick Fly

DRESSING

Hook	Mustad 38941 long shank sizes 12–14
Thread	Black pre-waxed
Tail	None
Body	Green-dyed raffia and green silk
Thorax	Yellow or green silk
Hackle	Ginger hen

METHOD

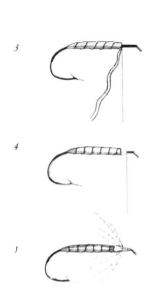

Step 1　Take the tying thread down the shank and there tie in a length of green silk and a strip of green raffia about ⅛ in in width.

Step 2　Take the thread back to the point shown and follow this with the green silk underbody. Tie off and cut away surplus silk. Endeavour to taper this underbody.

Step 3　Now wrap the silk with the raffia and tie off and remove any excess raffia. It is always a good idea to coat the raffia with clear varnish; this extends the life of the fly. At this point tie in the length of yellow or cream silk.

Step 4　Form the thorax of the fly (this is really the body of the larva projecting out of the case). Cut off any excess silk.

Step 5　Now wind on a few turns of hackle to simulate the legs. Finish the fly with a whip finish and a dab of varnish.

THE LATEX LARVA

There are a number of different flies using latex as the main body ingredient. I devised this one to imitate the non-case-making larvae of the *Rhyacophila* and *Hydropsyche*. I have one account of a tyro angler who took the wrong box of flies on a salmon-fishing trip in Scotland. Knowing no better, he put on one of these flies and managed to hook and land two salmon. No one had told him he was using the wrong fly and probably to this day he is none the wiser.

In this fly I have used ostrich herl as the breathing apparatus, in the form of a rib. Ostrich herl is notoriously fragile. I have found it better to wind on the ostrich herl first, then wrap with the latex, allowing the ostrich to project at intervals along the hook. All latex flies have a very short 'shelf life'; after a little while the latex tends to perish. This fly, like many of the larval imitations, can be weighted with copper or lead wire in order to get it down in the water to where the trout are likely to be.

DRESSING

Hook	Mustad 37160 sizes 10–12 or Partridge Caddis Hook size 8 or Tiemco TMC200 sizes 8–12
Thread	Black or brown pre-waxed
Tail	None
Body	Cream or green latex strip
Rib	Olive or cream ostrich herl
Thorax	Dark brown seal's fur or substitute
Hackle	Brown partridge hackle

Latex Larva

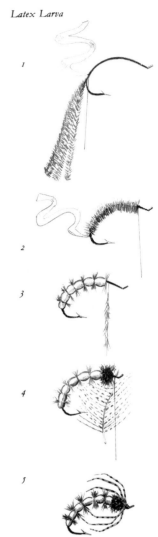

METHOD

Step 1   Take the thread down the hook. Now tie in a strip of latex approximately ⅛ in wide, and three or four strands of ostrich herl.

Step 2   Return the thread back along the shank to the point shown and then twist the ostrich herl into a rope and wind it up the shank. Tie off and cut away any surplus ostrich herl.

Step 3   Now wind the latex up the shank, covering the ostrich herl, but leaving gaps so that the herl protrudes in more or less equal segments. At this point dub a pinch of brown fur onto the tying thread.

Step 4   Form a thorax with the fur and tie in a partridge hackle by the point.

Step 5   Wind on the hackle. Two or three turns will be sufficient. Finish with a neat small head, whip finish and varnish. The fly is now complete. If a weighted pattern is required, wind lead or copper wire down the shank before applying the body materials. If the weight is applied in the area before the eye of the hook, under what will be the thoracic area, the fly will have a diving effect which can be quite attractive to the trout.

THE SAND CADDIS

There are a number of patterns imitating a caddis larva in a case made of grains of sand. I tied up a number of these a few years ago and, quite coincidentally, so did the late Richard Walker. It is his pattern that I give here. The fly is tied in the same way as the stick fly patterns above, but after the body has been put on it is coated in Vycoat or a similar product, then rolled in fine sand. It is then allowed to dry before proceeding with the next stage in the dressing. Richard Walker maintained that this pattern should be fished by being trundled along the bottom.

Pebble Caddis

DRESSING

Hook	Mustad long shank 79580 size 10
Thread	Black pre-waxed
Trail	None
Body	Cream or white floss coated as described above
Thorax	Amber or green wool
Hackle	Soft black hen hackle

Twig Caddis

THE TWIG CADDIS

There was a time in my fly-dressing career, such as it was, when I feel I took the art of realism too far. I indulged myself too much in direct representation to the detriment of the fish-catching potential of the fly. On occasions the flies looked so damned real I like to think they fooled rather than tempted the fish. Don't ask about my excuses when I failed to catch a fish on some of them.

This was not the case with this pattern. This was one of my flights of fancy that did actually catch a few trout, so I feel justified in including it here. It represents those caddis larvae that use vegetable matter to construct their cases. It is tied in the same way as the last pattern but, instead of coating in sand, little irregular bits of natural, brown and green raffia are stuck onto the body. When dry, a coat of clear varnish extends the life of the fly. This fly is also better if pre-weighted with lead or copper wire, in order to get it down to where the trout are.

THE DRESSING

Hook	Mustad 79580 sizes 10–12
Thread	Brown or black pre-waxed
Body	White, cream or green silk, onto which are stuck pieces of cut raffia or a similar product (one could use natural leaves, etc.). One or two tiny twigs are added for realism
Thorax	White, cream or brown silk or wool
Hackle	(optional) Light red hen

Sand Caddis

THE PEBBLE CADDIS

Now I have to admit that this pattern was a failure – not that I did not catch fish with it, no, but it was nigh on impossible to cast. I stuck to the body, by means of Araldite adhesive, small bits of gravel and pebbles from my aquarium. I must admit that in the vice it looked so realistic. I could have eaten it myself, but, as I say, it was a ton weight to cast. Since then I have found that some (unused!) cat litter solves the 'too heavy' problem. Tie the fly up exactly as the last pattern but substitute cat litter for the raffia. (Some types of cat litter are lighter than others. Choose the lightest, then you will at least have a caddis pattern you can cast.)

THE DRESSING

Hook	Mustad 79580 sizes 10–12
Thread	Brown or black pre-waxed
Body	White, green or cream silk covered with cat litter
Thorax	Brown silk or wool
Hackle	A few wisps of light red hen hackle

HYDROPSYCHE (MARBLED)

Moser's Hydropsyche

Roman Moser of Austria is one of Europe's most innovative fly dressers. He provided me with many patterns for my last book on international flies, *Fly Patterns*. Among the flies he sent was an excellent pattern tied to represent the larvae of the species *Hydropsyche*. The materials used in the tying were, in the main, modern products supplied by the fly-fishing company Traun River Products of Siegsdorf, West Germany.

DRESSING

Hook	Mustad 79580 size 10
Thread	Black or brown
Tail	Grey downy feathers from the base of a partridge hackle
Body	Body gill substitute with light grey wool
Back	Brown latex marked with a black marker pen
Hackle	Sparse false hackle of brown partridge
Head	Dubbed squirrel body fur

Apart from the Marbled *Hydropsyche*, Roman Moser has a number of other patterns to represent various other *Hydropsyche* species. All of his patterns are used on the fabled River Traun where the sedge in all its stages is considered to be a very important fly. His other patterns for this family are as follows.

HYDROPSYCHE (NO. 2)

DRESSING

Hook	Mustad 79580 sizes 10–12
Thread	Brown pre-waxed
Tail	Short tuft of yellow fluffy feather fibre

Body	Fine olive chenille (Moser uses a special chenille called Kaktus Chenille from Traun River Products)
Thorax	Dark brown Antron

HYDROPSYCHE (NO. 3)

DRESSING

Hook	Mustad 79580 sizes 10–12
Thread	Brown pre-waxed
Tail	Short tuft of grey fluffy feather fibre
Body	Dyed-olive hare's ear dubbing
Thorax	Yellow-dyed hare's ear with brown latex over
Hackle	Sparse black cock hackle to simulate legs

Another of Roman Moser's uncased caddis larva imitations is his version of the *Rhyacophila* species.

RHYACOPHILA

DRESSING

Hook	Mustad 79850 size 10
Thread	Brown pre-waxed
Tail	Short tuft of white fluffy feather fibre
Underbody	Yellowish-coloured body gill material
Back	Green Raffene
Belly	Yellow Raffene
Rib	Brown thread
Thorax	Mixed brown polypropylene dubbing and deer hair, brown Raffene over this

Moser has not ignored the cased larvae. He does not resort, as I have done, to sticking pieces of various substances onto the body of the fly, but uses a variety of modern materials to achieve the cased effect.

MOSER'S PEBBLE CASE LARVA

DRESSING

Hook	Mustad 79580 sizes 10–12
Thread	Brown pre-waxed
Body	Greyish-tan chenille
Thorax & head	Mixed deer hair and brown polypropylene dubbing

MOSER'S PLANT CASE LARVA

DRESSING

Hook	Mustad 79580 sizes 10–12
Thread	Brown pre-waxed
Body	Mixed light brown polypropylene dubbing and deer hair, clipped
Thorax	Dyed-yellow hare's ear with brown latex over the top
Hackle	Clipped sparse black cock to simulate legs

THE CASED CADDIS

One of the most skilful fly-dressers of recent times in Britain must be Bob Carnhill. His work has appeared every month in the magazine *Trout Fisherman*. Among the many patterns he has created is one tie to imitate the caddis larva in its case. This fly uses natural hare's fur as the body medium, as does a similar fly tied quite independently by Darrel. Martin of Tacoma, USA, a pattern I give on page 37.

DRESSING

Hook	Mustad 38941. Sizes 10–12
Thread	Black pre-waxed
Body	Hare's fur, three-quarters of the hook shank
Rib	Silver wire
Thorax	White swan herl (this is not, in essence, a thorax as such but represents the larva's body projecting out of the case)
Hackle	Small black hen

It is recommended that this pattern is weighted with lead wire.

THE CADDIS LARVA

In my opinion, one of the important influences on modern fly-dressing entomology in the last 30 years must be the writer C. F. Walker. His books on chalk-stream and also on lake flies have formulated opinion for many of today's fly tiers. He thought it fitting to have an imitation of the larval stage of the sedge which he called quite simply Caddis Larva. His particular pattern imitated a species not given earlier. The species Commander Walker had in mind was the sedge *Holocentropus dubius*, a non-case-making species, which hatches out into a medium-sized sedge with darkish brown wings spotted with paler yellow/brown spots. This sedge is quite a common species, in fact it was given by David Jacques in his list of identified species from Two Lakes in Hampshire. It is on the wing from May until September.

DRESSING

Hook	Mustad 79580 sizes 12–14 (Walker gave odd sizes which are no longer available)
Thread	Black or brown pre-waxed
Body	Three-quarters yellow seal's fur, one-quarter green seal's fur
Rib	Gold tinsel
Hackle	Woodcock under covert
Head	Cock pheasant tail fibres

Walker recommends the fly be weighted with copper or lead wire.

Franko's Nymph

FRANKO'S NYMPH

I was shown this pattern by Gorjan Franko of Tolmin in the fabulous Soca valley in Slovenia, Yugoslavia. Many of the rivers in that area have very good hatches of all species of sedge. This fly imitates rather well a larva of the *Rhyacophila* genus.

DRESSING

Hook	Mustad 79580 or similar sizes 10–12
Thread	Brown pre-waxed
Body	Two-thirds cream-coloured fur, one-third brown fur
Rib	Gold or silver
Hackle	Brown partridge hackle (optional)

This fly, like the other flies, can be weighted, but rules of fishing on the River Soca forbid this method, for it has proved too killing for both grayling and the indigenous trout of that area, the marbled trout (*Salmo marmoratus cuvier*). The fly fishermen of the Tolmin Club are concerned to preserve their fish stocks and do not like too many fish returning back over the borders to Austria and Italy in the bottom of deep freeze containers.

The United States can provide us with many patterns to represent the larval stage of the sedge. In fact, the Americans seldom refer to this insect as a sedge, using the term caddis for both larval and winged stages. I have selected but a few of the patterns listed by the American fly tiers – to give them all would take up most of a book. The first of these flies is a well-tried pattern of long standing. It is normally tied on normal shank hooks. On such hooks, to my mind, it resembles a pupa and not a larva, but tied on a longer-shanked

hook one can believe it to be a caddis larva. I refer to the pattern
known as the Breadcrust.

This standard American pattern is used to represent a species of
uncased caddis. As I have said, it was normally tied on conventional
hooks but Leiser and Solomon in their book *The Caddis and the
Angler* recommend the fly be tied up on the old English bait hook,
Mustad 37160.

THE BREADCRUST

Breadcrust

DRESSING

Hook	Mustad 38941 or as stated above
Thread	Black pre-waxed
Body	Orange floss
Rib	Hackle stalk from a dark brown cock feather
Hackle	Grizzle hen

The fly can also be tied up using a green or cream floss body, and
can, if so desired, be pre-weighted.

The next fly from the States represents a cased caddis, a similar
pattern to the caddis Izaak Walton called a hedgehog. It is a fair
representation of the European caddis *Limnephilus rhombicus* or the
American genus *Platycentropus*.

THE STRAWMAN NYMPH

Strawman Nymph

This is an extremely easy fly to tie. It uses deer body hair spun onto
the hook and then carelessly trimmed to resemble the case of the
caddis that forms its shelter from twigs sticking out in all directions.
It is necessary to pre-weight this pattern.

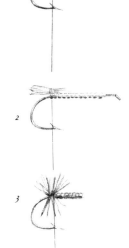

DRESSING

Hook	Mustad 79580 sizes 8–12
Thread	Black or brown pre-waxed
Body	Roughly clipped deer hair
Rib	Yellow silk (optional)
Hackle	None

The pattern is credited to Paul Young. Ray Bergman, in his book
Trout, gives this pattern with a tail of grey-speckled mallard fibres.
Nowadays this is generally omitted.

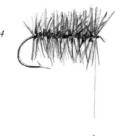

4

5

Hare Caddis

1 *2*

3

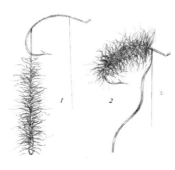

4

5

METHOD

Step 1 Pre-weight the hook with lead or copper wire and take the tying thread down the shank.

Step 2 Cut off a small bunch of deer hair and, with the soft loop method, take the thread over the hair and pull the thread tight.

Step 3 The deer hair should spin around the shank as in the drawing.

Step 4 Continue to spin on bunches of hair until the whole shank is full.

Step 5 Finish off the fly with the usual whip finish and varnish. Clip the deer hair to shape – the more ragged the better.

THE HARE CADDIS

This pattern was created by Darrel Martin of Tacoma, Washington State in the Pacific North West. It is similar in many respects to the cased caddis pattern of Bob Carnill. However, Darrel takes it a stage further and provides the imitation with a definite head complete with eyes. He also uses the curved caddis-type hook instead of the straight long shank.

DRESSING

Hook	Partridge Caddis Hook size 8, or Mustad 37160 size 12
Thread	Black pre-waxed
Body	Dubbed hare's fur
Rib	None
Thorax	Yellow floss
Hackle	Sparse brown partridge
Head	Black polypropylene with burnt nylon for eyes

METHOD

Step 1 Take the tying thread down the hook shank and there tie in a loop of waxed thread. Return the tying thread back up the shank. Place some hare's fur into the waxed loop and spin or twist.

Step 2 Form the abdomen by winding on the fur-laden loop. Applying dubbing by means of the waxed loop gives a much hairier body than dubbing straight onto the tying thread. Tie in the length of floss silk.

Step 3 Form the yellow portion of the body and tie in the partridge hackle. in order to get a sparse hackle, remove all the fibres from one side of the partridge feather before tying in by the tip.

Step 4 Cut about ½ in of clear nylon of about 10 lb strength and, holding it in a pair of tweezers or pliers, melt both ends with a flame to form two little beads. Tie this piece of beaded nylon on top of the hook after the hackle. Dub some black polypropylene fur onto the tying thread.

Step 5   Wind on the polypropylene to form the head, wrapping in between the eyes. Finish the fly in the usual way. Like all the pupa patterns, this fly can be pre-weighted.

With the many species of Trichoptera found in the USA, it is little wonder that they have more caddis imitations than the rest of the fly-fishing countries put together. In the past, with very few exceptions, little interest has been shown in Europe in imitating the caddis larva. This may well be due to the fact that the natural larvae themselves were often used as a bait and therefore the need to imitate the creature was not a priority. I believe, also, that the importance of the sedge family as a whole was very much underestimated by earlier writers. Too much emphasis was, and to a certain extent still is, placed on the Ephemerids, the sedges seemingly playing a secondary role. The next larva imitation uses skunk tail hair to achieve the effect of a cased caddis.

Skunk Hair Caddis

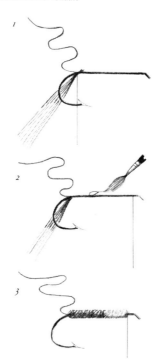

THE SKUNK HAIR CADDIS
This pattern has been devised to imitate a genus found in the USA, namely *Hesperophylax*, a Limnephilid from the western states.

DRESSING

Hook	Mustad 38941 sizes 8–10
Thread	Black pre-waxed
Body	Natural skunk tail, the black portion must be at least 4 in long
Rib	Copper wire
Hackle	Small black hen

METHOD

Step 1   Take the thread down the hook and there tie in a bunch of skunk hair, about 4 mm in thickness, by the black tips. Also tie in a length of copper wire.

Step 2   Return the thread back down the shank leaving room for the head and the hackle. Coat the thread on the hook with varnish.

Step 3   Twist the skunk hair into a rope and twist it in a clockwise motion around the shank. Tie off securely and cut off any surplus hair.

Step 4 Wind on the copper wire rib anti-clockwise. Tie off and cut off any surplus wire.

Step 5 Tie in and wind a small black hen hackle. Finish the fly with a neat head and whip finish. Varnish the head and the fly is now complete. Like all larval patterns, this fly can be pre-weighted with lead or copper wire.

Halford's Grannom Larva

THE GRANNOM LARVA

I thought it fitting, if not a little paradoxical, to include a larval pattern devised by the doyen of dry fly fishing, Frederic Maurice Halford. If a dry fly zealot like Halford thought it useful to have a copy of a caddis larva then who am I not to give his pattern here. He said that the trout on the Houghton stretch of the Test fed ravenously on the larvae and ignored the adults. The following fly was copied from a Grannom larva taken from a trout's stomach in 1884.

DRESSING

Hook	Mustad 94841 sizes 10–12
Thread	Brown pre-waxed
Body	Pea-green floss
Rib	Peacock quill dyed insect-green
Wing	A tip of a brown partridge hackle
Hackle	Rusty-dun cock hackle

It would appear that Halford ignored the case of this larva.

The Spanish are renowned fly fishermen. The following two patterns were sent to me by Luis Anntunez of Madrid, a most skilful fly fisherman and fly dresser.

DEEP CADDIS LARVA (SPANISH)

Hook	Mustad 94840 sizes 8–10 weighted with copper wire
Thread	Black pre-waxed
Body	Hare's fur
Rib	Black thread
Hackle	Short tuft of grey hackle fibres beneath the hook
Thorax	Dark brown fur

RHYACOPHILA LARVA (SPANISH)

Hook	Mustad 94840 sizes 10–14 weighted with copper wire

Thread	Black pre-waxed
Body	Green latex
Rib	Bronze peacock herl
Head	Peacock herl

To finish off this collection of caddis imitations, let us look at a couple of patterns from the antipodes and from New Zealand in particular. The first is called the Horn Caddis and is a very simple pattern to tie up. The other is a little more complex as it requires a detached body. Both are tied on conventional hooks, but there is nothing to stop you using long-shanked hooks for both patterns. The necessity for using a detached body no longer exists.

Rhyacophila Larva

THE HORN CADDIS

An effective pattern from the fast flowing rivers of South Island in New Zealand. Pre-weight the fly with copper wire, for this pattern must be fished as close to the bottom as possible.

DRESSING

Hook	Mustad 94841 sizes 10–14 (can also be tied on long shank hooks)
Thread	Grey or black pre-waxed
Body	Grey darning wool
Rib	Silver wire
Collar	White wool
Hackle	None as such, but a few fibres of grizzle hackle projecting out of the front to simulate the legs of the larva.

Horn Caddis

The body of this pattern is usually coated with clear varnish. I would imagine that this could well be an effective pattern for grayling for it has a great similarity to Sawyer's Grayling Bug; both use darning wool as the main ingredient.

BRAGG'S CADDIS LARVA

This pattern was created by the New Zealand fly tier and fisherman R. K. Bragg and was given in Keith Draper's book, *Trout Flies in New Zealand*. This pattern was originally tied as a detached bodied fly but I have converted the pattern to a long shank hook. According to Draper the pattern was tied to imitate a cased caddis called *Olinga feredayi* (not found in Europe as far as I can see), but its coloration

would be more in keeping with a free-swimming caddis such as *Rhyacophila* or *Hydropsyche* in the UK.

DRESSING

Hook	Mustad 9671 sizes 10–14 (this hook is a good hook for all types of nymph, being a standard hook with twice the extra length in the shank)
Thread	Yellow or black pre-waxed
Body	Golden yellow floss silk
Rib	Fluorescent yellow silk
Hackle	Small grizzle hackle dyed yellowish-brown

In Walton's day it was thought that the caddis larva turned into a mayfly. On the fifth day of Walton's discourse, our 'Piscator', on approaching the village of Tottenham, turned to his companion and said, 'Well, scholar I have held you too long about these caddis.'

This may also apply to me, so let us look at the fishing.

CHAPTER SIX
FISHING THE CADDIS LARVA

Perhaps the soundest advice I was ever given regarding fishing, was to treat the fly at the end of the line as a living creature. The fly must look alive; it should behave as near as possible like the real creature it is imitating. It must, of course, look attractive to the trout and, above all, it must appear as food to our quarry. If it does none of these things then we are not likely to take any fish on it. Fish are perhaps not the brightest of creatures in the brain stakes, but neither are they completely stupid. They have been given a degree of animal instinct and certainly they are wary of the unnatural. They can be easily spooked and big trout do not get to be big trout if they are unaware of something alien in their vicinity.

An angler must couple an attractive fly with correct presentation. You can cast the most attractive fly in the world, but if it does not appear natural to the feeding fish then you can safely say you are wasting your time. So in the instance of the caddis, what must we try to do? Firstly, we must ask ourselves, 'Where will the trout find the caddis larva?' Well, as I have previously stated, the most likely area is down on the bottom. There are, of course, exceptions. Some species will be active in weed beds and therefore these larvae will be found higher up in the water, clinging to and feeding upon the tresses of weed. Again, we have the *Triaenodes* bicolor sedge actively swimming in open water, albeit close to weedy areas. So we have three possible areas of presentation. The bulk of caddis will be down near the bottom; a percentage will be in the weed beds and can fall victim to foraging trout which make forays into the weed for such insect delicacies; finally, on still water close to the weedy margins, we have the free-swimming variety.

The next question we must ask is, 'When do we fish a caddis larvae?' The answer may appear to be a little obvious, but I would fish such a fly when I could see no evidence that the trout were

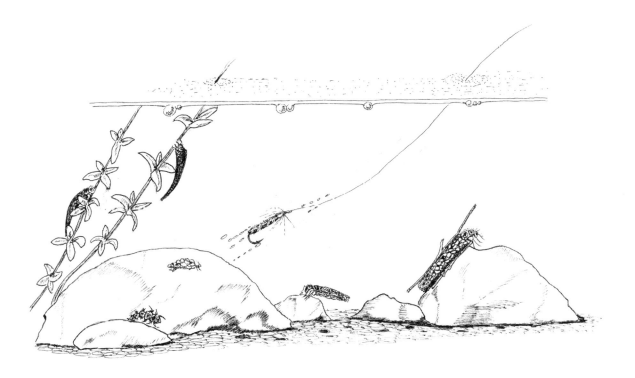

feeding on anything else. A little basic? Well of course it is. If trout are not rising to the surface to take flies on top, they must be feeding on something else. The largest percentage of food taken by a trout is taken sub-surface, so all the dry flies in the world will be of little use if our friend the trout is preoccupied in taking a nymph or, in our case here, a caddis larva.

Now, the next stage requires a little bit of luck or skill, for we need to take a fish in order to investigate its stomach contents. If there are caddis in the autopsy then you can pat yourself on the back. If there are no caddis all is not lost, for if the contents show an amalgam of different creatures, then you can assume that the trout is on the lookout for anything edible and the caddis fly that you tempt it with will be as good as any other fly to try in the circumstances. In clear crystal water it may be possible actually to see the fish forage on the bottom for caddis, but most of the time this is not likely.

One could ask the question, 'How do you know there are any caddis larvae in the water?' Well, it would be a strange water indeed that did not have its indigenous caddis, but if you do not believe me have a look for yourselves. Pick a few rocks out of the water or pull out a bunch of weed and look. This can be a little more difficult on a reservoir, I admit, but look at the margins of such water. Quite often, in the washed-up flotsam, one can find the cases of various species of sedge. But enough of the reasons why, let us now look at some of the mechanics of 'how'.

I have often read, in short preambles to fly patterns representing caddis larvae, that they should be fished as a nymph. 'Fished as a nymph'! What nymph? An Ephemerid? A damsel nymph? Or what? I would give the short answer that it is not fished as a nymph but more as a bottom crawler, not as a creature rising in the main body of the water prior to hatching at the surface. With the exception of the *Triaenodes* species, most of the larvae we are likely to come across are not active swimmers; they lumber about the bottom or climb weedy patches with the slow deliberation of an Amazonian sloth. The only time you will encounter them moving at speed is when they have lost their hold and have been swept away by the current. As your fly is in the same water it will be travelling at almost the same speed. If left alone, your fly and the natural one will behave as one in the hurly burly of the water, providing you do not let your line drag in the current.

There has been a lot of discussion as to what is the correct size of rod for fishing rivers. Do you fish a short rod or do you go to the other extreme and fish with something quite long? I would always advise any angler to fish with a rod he is happy with. If you have to settle on one rod then a rod between $8\frac{1}{2}$–9 ft would satisfy most needs. There are some who feel that a short 7–$7\frac{1}{2}$-ft light rod is a sporting rod to use on rivers. I have one which I use on small streams, but on larger rivers it has the drawback of making me work hard to project line. I remember on one occasion I was fishing a river to rising fish; they were rising, as it happens, to ovipositing sedges. Another angler, who was not really aware of angling etiquette, walked up the bank and stood not more that 10 yd from me; only a large bush separated him from me. In front was this constantly rising trout. When fish are rising to such female sedges they often miss them in their eagerness to take and if you can get your fly into the ring of the rise the trout will often turn and take your pattern. That was exactly what happened on that occasion. One false cast with my 9-ft rod sent my fly out into the vicinity of the rising fish. It turned in a flash and I hooked it. In the meantime the gentleman behind the bush, with a 7-ft rod, was still trying to aerialise line in order to get his fly somewhere near the fish. It was a case when a longer rod proved its worth.

In fishing caddis imitations we must remember that for most of the time we will be fishing weighted flies, and in some instances they will be heavily weighted. If we are using a leader that is too long, our fly will be acting as a pendulum on the back cast. You will know when this happens, for if your fly has not hit you on the back of the neck or on some other part of your anatomy you will see it following your fly line in a most erratic manner, so I would use a leader approximately the length of the rod – 9–10 ft for a 9-ft rod and $8\frac{1}{2}$–9 ft for the rod of $8\frac{1}{2}$ ft. The point of the leader must be of sufficient strength to handle the fly. If it is too light then our heavy caddis pattern will be flicked off, and as we expect to fish our artificial down on the bottom, bumping its way over the stones and gravel, a leader point of about 5 lb breaking strength would be the strength I would use; anything less and we would be courting disaster. As for the fly line, on rivers I use mainly a floating line, sometimes a sink tip or an intermediate. For stillwater I sometimes resort to a much faster sinking line.

FISHING THE CADDIS LARVAE IN STILLWATER

Fishing caddis larvae in lakes and reservoirs is ideally suited to bank angling rather than from a boat. With very few exceptions, the natural caddis is found close to the margins in the shallower water in the vicinity of weedy areas, many of them browsing on such vegetation. You will also find caddis on dam walls feeding on the algaeic matter on the concrete. Old roadways are also good areas for caddis larvae as are sunken hedgerows and old treelines. These vestiges of former times soon get coated in various forms of algae, making them ideal pastures for many aquatic larvae, not only the caddis. Wherever streams or water-filled ditches enter a reservoir or lake, you will find caddis larvae and in some instances some caddis could be local to that particular place. Even if you are fishing some other fly, not the caddis, all the areas mentioned are considered good fish holding spots.

There is no need to use fast sinking, high density lines; you will soon get caught up on the bottom if you do. Floating, sink tip or intermediate lines are the best ones to use from the bank. What I said earlier regarding leader length still holds true; you are in trouble if your leader is too long with the weighted flies. If using non-weighted patterns and sinking/sink tip lines, then, of course, a longer leader can be used. A long leader can often be an advantage in bank fishing. Many of our leading bank fishermen advocate the use of ultra-long leaders and the only advice I can add to this is to say fish with a leader as long as you, your rod and the prevailing weather conditions allow. I have found it nigh on impossible to fish with a 20-ft leader into the teeth of a strong wind, and I suspect many of those who advocate the long leader find equal difficulty. With the exception of the free-swimming *bicolor* sedge, which swims quite actively in the main body of the water, all other caddis larvae imitations should be fished as slowly as possible, close to the bottom. In some cases an effective method is to cast out and allow the fly to swing round with the natural flow of the water. This movement of the fly emulates the behaviour of a caddis swept away from its hold. The aftermath of windy conditions can also be a good time to fish caddis larvae imitations, for if the wind has stirred up the mud along the shoreline then, without doubt, among the washed-out food there will be caddis. In such situations boat anglers may find it beneficial to fish the margin of this muddy area, for trout wait on the fringes of coloured water, picking up the tasty morsels dislodged from the reservoir or lake bottom.

FISHING THE CADDIS IN RIVERS AND STREAMS

The methods and ethics of fishing some streams and rivers have always been open to debate. The Victorian fly fishermen, who plied their art or craft on the hallowed waters of the southern chalk streams, laid down a set of guidelines which they considered to be the correct and *only* method of taking trout from such waters. The legacy of 'dry fly only' is still with us, as is the dictum of fishing upstream. I still know of some waters in Hampshire where the rule 'dry fly fished upstream' is strictly applied and where use of a nymph means immediate expulsion from the water. These rules and regulations come pretty hard to a Welshman whose first attempts with a fly rod were fishing wild turbulent streams in Wales, always with a wet fly and inevitably downstream. One can, to a degree, understand the logic, and to a certain extent appreciate the sporting nature of such rules. Even the rawest beginner knows that for most of the time the fish face upstream and the best way to catch them is to come up behind them. Therefore, if on certain waters these regulations still apply then they should be complied with and accepted as being the only method for that water. If you are not allowed to use a nymph, then you can forget fishing the caddis larva.

That great angler and writer, Skues, who fished such rivers in Hampshire as the Itchen, brought down about his head the wrath of the angling gods when he developed and fished his 'wet' nymph patterns after appreciating the value of North Country flies fished in the traditional manner in the northern counties. His then-revolutionary methods gave great offence and caused an indignation bordering on apoplexy among his peers. He was considered no better than a poacher – or worse, perhaps even a fishmonger – because of his undoubted success with his new-fangled nymphs.

I remember once fishing a river where all the anglers were hell bent on fishing tiny dry flies upstream – they had become the Spanish personifications of Halford. The river was the Tormes in central Spain. If ever a water cried out for an across-stream nymph it was this river, but my Spanish friends had, for some reason or another, adopted an English chalk-stream method. I doubt if their cousins, fishing some of the wilder rivers that tumble out of the Pyrenees, would have fished in the same way.

The River Unec (pronounced Oonetz) flows out of a giant cave near the village of Plannina south east of Ljubljana in Slovenia. It is a pure chalk stream to rival any chalk stream in the south of England, and yet if you try to catch trout or grayling by upstream methods on dry fly or emerging nymph, you will be decidedly unsuccessful. Do not ask me why, I do not know. I have tried and so have my fishing friends, and all of us soon resort to fishing across and down to the rising fish. If it had been just me alone who experienced this phenomenon, I would have put it down to my obvious lack of skill, but I have fished here in the company of top chalk-stream anglers of various nationalities and their experiences have been the same as mine.

I only mention the question of upstream fishing because if this rule applies to the water you fish, then the use of a caddis larva imitation is going to be limited. In fishing such imitations it is going to be necessary to fish both up and down as well as across. So let us deal first with such waters where this upstream rule applies. They will inevitably be chalk streams and stretches of such rivers where nymph fishing is allowed. The caddis larvae will be found right throughout the river system, some of the obvious places being among the prolific weed beds found in these high alkaline waters. Trout do make forays into such areas to flush out shrimps, waterlice, Ephemerid and damsel nymphs and also various species of caddis larvae. The larvae are also to be found in the vicinity of manmade objects such as wooden and concrete groynes and the walls of weirs where algae and weed clothe the stone or brickwork like a green silk mandarin's beard. Perhaps the most effective method on such waters is to seek out the small weirs where the water is usually a little deeper than in the river proper, due to the natural scouring that the constant fall of water creates.

If you cast your heavy weighted caddis larva up into such areas, it is unusual not to take a fish from such hot spots. Let the water do the work for you. Your fly is held for some time in the conflicting currents of such mini-weirs. Just keep a tight line and strike at any movement or hesitance in the fly line. This is true for any type of weighted fly, not just a caddis imitation.

Where wading is permissible, cast upstream into the clear areas between the flowing water weed tresses. Trout that shelter beneath the fronds of weed will often slide out to intercept a tempting morsel as it is swept past. On rivers where any method of fly fishing is allowed, and there is no restriction on wading or type of fly, etc., then the angler has more options open to him or her.

As I have explained earlier, the natural caddis is generally a bottom dweller. It is not an active swimmer darting from stone to stone or from the riverbed to the surface; it is only found in the main body of the water if it has been swept away by accident. As far as the trout is concerned, this must be classed as serendipitous food. It is not a normal occurrence, and while the trout will happily accept such free-swimming morsels, it is more likely to be found foraging for the larvae on the bottom or around aquatic vegetation. In his book, *Caddisflies*, Gary LaFontaine states that even though the trout's mouth is not really built for bottom feeding, it will still attempt to take caddis larvae from rocks and stones. I have not seen this myself, but do not doubt that it happens. On the other hand, I have seen trout make forays into weed, swing back into open water and drop back down to see what has been flushed out.

I have found the best way to cast these weighted caddis is to cast up and across the river and allow the fly to come down, bumping the bottom. For this the rod is held aloft and follows the fly line and leader in a sweeping action. Before the line starts to drag, lift off and repeat. Fish all the likely trout-holding areas and be prepared to strike at a moment's hesitation in the fly line. This could mean that a trout has taken your fly (on the other hand, you could be caught up on a rock – it's the chance you take).

The topography of the water and position of a feeding fish sometimes require you to fish downstream. Solomon and Leiser, in their book *The Caddis & the Angler*, suggest one cast downstream and then feed out more line through the rings. They recommend one to strip off 40–50 ft of line from the reel, cast out 30 ft, feed the remainder through the rings, then walk downstream. I find this method not too successful. It may well be me, but the further I am from the hook the less chance I have of hooking the fish, especially downstream, for by the time a take registers with me the fish is long gone. It either takes the fly and rejects it, or, because of the length of line I had out, I have failed to set the hook against the flow of the river. I still prefer to cast up and across and sweep my fly downstream. When you cast you can lay a line down with a wiggle in it by short-waving the rod with a mere left and right flick of the wrist, just before the line hits the water. This more or less pre-mends the line, giving the fly time to sink further down, and it retards the drag on the line. I do not advocate the use of caddis larvae imitations as some new panacea method of taking trout. The use of such flies is usually confined to times when there appears to be no other insect activity on the water. To seek out a trout by this means then is as good as any.

CHAPTER SEVEN
IMITATIONS
OF THE PUPA

This is the most vulnerable time for the sedge, for it is now at the mercy of the trout, as well as other predators, as it rises from the apparent safety of its solid pupal case to seek the water surface in order to spread its new-found wings. While it is in its pupal case it is reasonably safe from predation for it is more or less quiescent, displaying no movement that might attract a trout, but once it has changed into its pre-adult form and released itself from its self-imposed imprisonment, then danger looms large for the infant sedge. So it is little wonder that the imitations of sedge pupae are legion and they are considered to be an important fly in the armoury of both stillwater and river fisherman.

Before the turn of the twentieth century little or no attention was paid to what we now consider to be an important fishing fly. The adult sedge has figured in the literature and the fly wallets of anglers since the days of Dame Juliana Berners, but of the humble pupa almost total ignorance is manifest. It has been the lot of the modern fly fisherman to convert this Cinderella of a fly into a certain belle of the angling ball.

If we draw a comparison between the Trichoptera and the Lepidoptera, then once a butterfly leaves its cocoon and expands its wings it is an adult. Surely this must also be true of the sedge? The metamorphosis occurs within the pupal chamber, but once it leaves this chamber it is to all intents and purposes an adult fly, albeit still under water and with its wings unexpanded and covered by a membrane of skin. Should we call the creature at this stage a pupa or perhaps an emerging adult? I think the question is open to debate.

In the selection of pupal patterns, I have endeavoured to encompass both early and modern flies, tied with both traditional and also modern manmade products. Many of the patterns will be similar and, furthermore, there will not be a lot to choose among any of them as far as fishing is concerned, but the old adage holds true – 'one man's meat is another man's poison'. We all have our particular favourites and frankly that is the story of fly dressing. It has progressed the way it has because of individual fly tiers' and anglers' preferences and interpretations.

Bells Amber Nymph

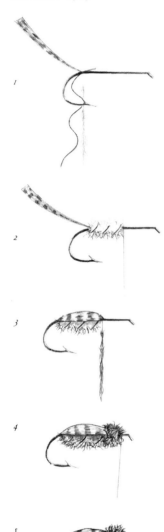

DR BELL'S AMBER NYMPHS

One of the first reservoirs opened for public trout fishing was the fine water of Blagdon, close to Bath and Bristol. Even the opening of further reservoirs in more recent times – waters such as Chew Valley – have not detracted from the popularity of Blagdon Water. At a time when most if not all of his contemporaries were fishing with conventional, traditional winged wet flies, Dr H. A. Bell created a whole series of flies based on the creatures he found in the stomach contents of caught fish. Among his fly selection were two patterns called the Amber Nymph; the first for fishing during the months of May and June; the second for fishing during July. Both flies are a fair representation of a sedge pupa.

THE LARGE AMBER NYMPH

DRESSING

Hook	Mustad 3904a size 10
Thread	Brown pre-waxed
Body	Amber seal's fur or floss silk
Rib	Black silk
Thorax	Brown seal's fur or floss silk
Wingcase	Grey-brown feather tied across the back and finishing before the thorax
Hackle	A few wisks of honey hackle beneath the hook

THE SMALL AMBER NYMPH

DRESSING

Hook   Mustad 3904a size 12

The rest of the fly is tied the same way as the Large Amber except that the thorax is tied with orange fur or floss instead of the brown. Both flies are tied fairly full.

METHOD

Step 1   After taking the thread down the hook, tie in a slip of grey-brown mottled feather, turkey or similar. Also at the same point tie in a length of black silk for the rib. Now dub the body fur onto the tying thread.

Step 2   Take the fur-laden thread up to the point shown, followed by the rib.

Step 3   Bring the feather fibre over the back. Tie off and remove surplus. Dub the thorax fur onto the tying thread.

Step 4   Wind on the fur-laden thread to form the thorax.

Step 5   Under the hook tie in a few honey cock hackle fibres. Form a head, whip finish, varnish and the fly is complete.

SWEET'S AMBER NYMPH

Lionel Sweet was, without doubt, one of the great legends of the River Usk, the famed river of the Welsh borders. Many years ago I spent a very happy evening in his company at a fly fishing dinner. He explained at length how, as a young man, he was trained as a sign writer and how he used his past training in the design of some of his fishing flies. One in particular he called his Amber Nymph. This fly uses a double rib. The black ribbing is used to emphasise the gold, making it stand out bold and clear, just as a signwriter places a shadow behind a letter for the same purpose.

DRESSING

Hook	Mustad 3904a sizes 10–14
Thread	Brown or orange pre-waxed
Body	Amber floss silk
Rib	Gold tinsel and black silk close behind the tinsel
Hackle	Light ginger cock tied sparse

METHOD

Step 1   Take the thread down the hook and at that point tie in a length of black tying thread and a length of fine oval gold tinsel.

Step 2   Return the tying thread up the shank to the position shown and there tie in a length of amber floss.

Step 3   Wind this floss down the shank and back again, forming a tapered body.

Step 4   Now first wind the gold rib up the body, then follow this with the black rib, right up against the gold.

Step 5   Finally wind on a few turns of light ginger hackle. Finish the fly with the usual whip finish and varnish.

Step by step: Sweet's Amber Nymph

THE JOHN GODDARD PUPA

John Goddard's contribution to our understanding of our sport is unquestioned. Both in his books and in his many articles he has been responsible for enlightening many of us as to the ways of the trout and also of the many ways of the trout's food, the aquatic insect. Among the many flies he has created are a series of simple sedge pupae patterns for use on stillwater. These flies are now considered to be standard patterns in the fly boxes of the reservoir angler.

DRESSING

Hook	Mustad long shank 9672 sizes 10–12
Thread	Brown pre-waxed
Body	Seal's fur, either cream, brown, olive or orange
Rib	Fine silver tinsel
Thorax	Dark brown condor herl substitute
Wingcase	Dark brown condor herl substitute
Hackle	Sparse, honey or rusty hen

Persuader

THE PERSUADER

John Goddard's other pattern which can be used as a sedge pupa, is his well-known reservoir fly the Persuader. Tied ostensibly as an attractor pattern, this fly works very well during a sedge hatch. This is due to its pupal shape and its brightness (the fish can see it).

DRESSING

Hook	Partridge Captain Hamilton L2a, Mustad 79672 sizes 8–10
Thread	Orange pre-waxed
Body	Approximately four or five strands of white ostrich herl
Rib	Fine silver oval tinsel
Thorax	Orange seal's fur
Wingcase	Turkey feather fibre (cock pheasant tail is as effective)

METHOD

Like Goddard's series of sedge pupae patterns, the Persuader is an extremely easy fly to tie.

Just tie in the ostrich herl and silver rib at the tail end of the hook. Form the ostrich herl body, followed by the rib. Tie in a slip of feather fibre for the wingcase.

Dub on the fur for the thorax. Form the thorax. Take the wingcase over the back. Tie off, remove excess feather fibre and finish the fly in the normal way.

THE TOM IVENS'S PATTERNS

Tom Ivens can best be described as the father of modern reservoir fishing. His book, *Still Water Fly-Fishing*, pioneered this branch of our sport. Among the fly patterns given by him are a number of nymphs of the broad spectrum type, some of which can be taken as sedge pupae. His best known fly is the famous Jersey Herd lure.

IVENS'S BROWN NYMPH

DRESSING

Hook	Partridge L2a Mustad 79672 sizes 8–10
Thread	Black or brown pre-waxed
Body	Dark brown ostrich herl
Rib	Oval gold tinsel
Horns	Two tips of peacock herl sloping backwards
Head	Peacock herl

IVENS'S GREEN NYMPH

DRESSING

Hook	Partridge L2a Mustad 79672 sizes 8–12
Thread	Green pre-waxed
Body	White floss, over-wrapped with pale green nylon
Hackle	Brown partridge hackle
Head	Peacock herl

IVENS'S GREEN AND YELLOW NYMPH

DRESSING

Hook	Partridge L2a Mustad 79672 sizes 10–12
Thread	Green pre-waxed
Body	In two halves: the rear green swan herl; the front portion yellow swan herl
Rib	None is the original but, as the feather fibre is delicate, I rib with fine gold wire
Head	Peacock herl

Step by step: Ivens's Brown and Green

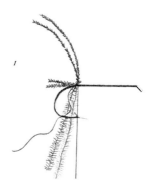

1

IVENS'S BROWN AND GREEN NYMPH

DRESSING

Hook	Partridge L2a Mustad 79672 sizes 8–10
Thread	Brown pre-waxed
Body	Olive and brown ostrich twisted together

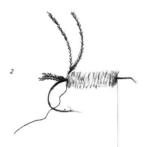

Rib	Oval gold tinsel
Back	Peacock herl, tied across the back, with the fibres extending beyond the hook as a tail
Head	Peacock herl

All these flies are simple to tie, so I feel it necessary to give instructions only for the this last one.

METHOD

Step 1 Take the thread down the hook and tie in two strands of peacock herl and a strand each of olive and brown ostrich herl. Tie the peacock so that it projects as a small tail. Also tie in the ribbing medium.

Step 2 Take the thread down the shank to the point shown. Twist the ostrich herl together into a rope and wind it up the shank to form the body.

Step 3 Wind on the rib, then take the peacock herl over the back. Tie off and cut away any surplus.

Step 4 Tie in two further strands of peacock herl and form a head. Complete the fly in the normal manner.

THE RICHARD WALKER SEDGE PUPAE

It is fitting that we include a selection of Richard Walker's sedge pupae patterns, for without doubt he must be considered one of Britain's finest all-round freshwater anglers. His untimely death from cancer a few years ago left a void in the potential literature of fly fishing. His few books were, alas, too few, and I, for one, feel there were many more to come. I had the pleasure of illustrating his last published book on flies, Dick Walker's *Modern Fly Dressings*.

THE SHORTHORN

This pupa represents the pupal stage in the life cycle of such species as the Brown or Black Silverhorn or any of the *Mystacides* species of sedge.

DRESSING

Hook	Mustad 3904a sizes 10–14
Thread	Brown pre-waxed
Body	Dark olive-brown feather fibre
Rib	Yellow tying thread
Thorax	Greeny-yellow or orange fluorescent wool
Wingcase	A strip of black lurex
Hackle	Brown partridge, tied in two bunches, flanking the body

THE LONGHORN

This pattern imitates the pupa of *Ocetis lacustris* or *O. ochracea*, common on many of the day-ticket reservoirs in Great Britain.

DRESSING

Hook	Mustad 3904a sizes 8–12 (sometimes tied on long shanks)
Thread	Pale yellow pre-waxed
Body	Amber wool two-thirds, chestnut wool front third. (Alternative body colour, sea-green wool instead of the amber)
Rib	Fine oval gold tinsel rear portion only
Hackle	Two turns of brown partridge hackle
Antennae	Two cock pheasant centre tail strands sloping over the back

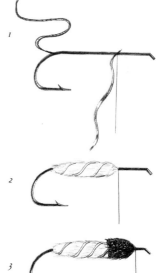

Walker Longhorn

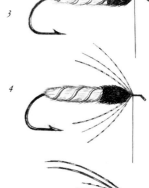

METHOD

Step 1 Take the tying thread down the hook and there tie in the ribbing tinsel. Take the thread two-thirds back along the shank and tie in the body wool.

Step 2 Form the body of the fly by winding the wool down the shank and back again. Remove surplus wool and wind on the rib.

Step 3 Tie in the brown wool and wind on to form the thorax of the fly.

Step 4 Tie in and wind on the partridge hackle.

Step 5 Tie in the two cock pheasant tail fibres so that they slope over the back. Finish the fly with a neat head. Whip finish and varnish and the fly is complete.

THE MEAD MILL SPECIAL

Richard Walker named this fly after Mead Mill on the River Test in Hampshire. It is tied up to represent a number of different aquatic creatures, among them a sedge pupa. This fly is generally pre-weighted with lead wire.

DRESSING

Hook	Partridge G3a or Mustad 79674 sizes 10–12
Thread	Olive pre-waxed
Body	Grass-green wool and fluorescent lime wool, chopped up and well mixed, used as dubbing
Rib	Fine oval gold tinsel
Back	Speckled turkey taken over the back
Antennae	Two fibres of the back material tied to slope back over the body

Mead Mill

Swannundaze Pupa

1

2

3

4

5

6

SWANNUNDAZE SEDGE PUPA

The material called Swannundaze was produced in the USA and offered to fly dressers by Frank A. Johnson of New Jersey. It is supplied in a whole range of colours, but the most useful are the transparent colours. The transparent yellow I use in this pattern of mine combines with the fluorescent underbody to give a very realistic abdomen. It has the effect of looking like the 'blood and guts' of the real insect. Whether the trout view it in the same way is highly debatable. Nevertheless, I, and many others, have caught plenty of trout with it, which shows at least that the fish treat it as something edible.

DRESSING

Hook	Partridge K4a sizes 8–10 or Mustad 37160 size 12
Thread	Brown pre-waxed
Underbody	Fluorescent red floss or fine wool
Overbody	Transparent yellow Swannundaze
Rib	A strand of peacock herl or ostrich herl
Thorax	Brown Antron or alternative dubbing
Wingcase	Cock pheasant tail fibres
Hackle	Brown partridge hackle
Antennae	Two cock pheasant tail fibres sloping backwards

METHOD

Step 1 Wind the thread down the hook and tie in the strand of peacock herl for the rib. Before tying in the Swannundaze, cut the material into a point and nibble the end slightly. This adds a few serrations which help to secure the material when you tie it in. Now tie the Swannundaze in, taking care to allow the curved side of the material to be uppermost. This provides the finished fly with a nice segmented abdomen. (The other side of the Swannundaze strip is flat.)

Step 2 Take the tying thread back along the shank to the point shown and tie in the length of red fluorescent floss.

Step 3 Take the floss down the shank and back again. Follow this with the Swannundaze to form the body. Cut off any surplus after tying off. Rib the Swannundaze with the peacock herl, allowing the herl to slip in between the turns of Swannundaze.

Step 4 Tie in a strip of cock pheasant tail on top of the hook. This will be the wingcase. Now tie in two strands of pheasant tail fibres on either side of the hook. Dub the brown fur dubbing onto the tying thread.

Step 5 Wind on the dubbed thread and form the thorax. Then wind on the partridge hackle about three turns.

Step 6 Take the cock pheasant tail fibres over the back and tie off. Cut away the surplus feather. This wingcase separates the hackle on either side of the hook. Form a neat head and finish the fly in the usual way.

Other pupae can be tied with the various Swannundaze colours. One should try to attain natural-looking colour combinations between the underbody and the overbody, using sombre colours such as brown, olive, cream and green.

THE LATEX PUPAE

Over the last fifteen years the use of latex sheet has become popular with fly dressers in the tying of various nymphs and pupae. Many fly dressers have used this medium in the creation of sedge pupae patterns. Flies tied up with this material can look extremely realistic but there are a couple of drawbacks concerning the versatility of latex. Firstly, latex does not have a long life; there is a tendency for it to perish. The other criticism lies in the fact that, on its own, it is a pretty inert material. It lacks life and in my opinion it should always be used in conjunction with more mobile 'alive' materials in order to give that integral life to the artificial fly. The fly that looks alive in water is the fly that is going to catch you a fish.

Just to set the record straight, the use of rubber-type materials in fly dressing goes back to the nineteenth century when they were used to construct detached bodies for dry flies. In those days they probably used gutta percha. I developed the following latex pattern from an American pattern, but added a little more movement to the fly, as I felt that too many of the existing latex patterns looked like nothing more than dead maggots. The material Spectraflash is a product sold by Traun River Products of West Germany.

THE LATEX SPECTRA PUPA

DRESSING

Hook	Mustad 31760 sizes 10–18 or Partridge K2b Yorkshire sedge hook sizes 8–16
Thread	Brown pre-waxed
Body	Cream-coloured latex
Wings	Two cut strips of Spectraflash
Thorax	Hare's fur including guard hairs
Wingcase	Cock pheasant tail fibres
Hackle	Brown partridge hackle
Antennae	Two cock pheasant tail fibres

Latex Spectra Pupa

METHOD

Step 1   First prepare the materials you are going to use. Cut a strip of latex about ⅛ in wide, and also prepare the wings to the shape shown.

Step 2   Take the thread down the shank and tie in the strip of latex.

Step 3   Return the thread up the shank. Wind the latex up the shank in overlapping turns. Do not pull it too tight in case you destroy the segmentation you are trying to achieve. Tie off the latex and cut off any excess.

Step 4   Tie in the two fibres of pheasant tail on both sides of the hook, then follow these with the wings, again on both sides of the hook as shown. Then, on top of the hook, tie in the feather fibre for the wingcase.

Step 5   Dub some of the hare's fur onto the tying thread and wind on to form the thorax.

Step 6   Wind on the partridge hackle and then bring the wingcase over to separate the hackle. Finish the fly in the usual way.

The gases trapped in the pupal skin of the sedge pupa can give the impression of a small creature encapsulated in a bubble of quick-silver as it progresses up to the surface. Gary LaFontaine imitated this property with the glistening manmade fibre Sparkle Yarn or Antron. He encompassed the body of his pupae patterns with this material, in order to give the impression of the real air-bubbled pupae. The flies reflected the available light in much the same way as a true air bubble. I have achieved the same temporary effect in some pupal patterns made of natural fur by weighting the fly with lead wire, dubbing on the fur, then rubbing in a small amount of petroleum jelly or silicone grease (not too much). This greased fur retains air bubbles which adhere to the grease within the hair itself. Periodic applications of the grease ensure a few bubbles of air will always adhere to the fur. But, I repeat, it must be on a weighted fly otherwise you will have a floating nymph.

Gary LaFontaine gives a number of colour combinations for his Sparkle Yarn pupae. He divides them up into two types: a deep pupa and an emergent pupa. The deep pupae patterns are weighted; the others are not. It is sufficient here just to give one pattern and list some of the other colour variations.

THE DEEP PUPA (BROWN AND YELLOW)

DRESSING

Hook	Mustad 94840 sizes 8–16
Thread	Brown pre-waxed
Underbody	Mixed russet or gold Sparkle Yarn and brown fur
Overbody	Russet or gold Sparkle Yarn
Hackle	Lemon wood duck along the sides
Head	Brown dubbed fur or dubbed brown marabou

Other flies in the series are: Brown and Green, Dark Grey, Ginger, Brown, Black, Grey and Yellow, Grey and Green. In fact you can easily devise your own colour combination to match the pupae common on the waters you fish.

THE EMERGENT PUPA (BROWN AND YELLOW)

Step by step: Emergent Pupa

DRESSING

Hook	Mustad 94840 sizes 8–16
Thread	Brown pre-waxed
Underbody	As Deep Pupa
Overbody	As Deep Pupa
Wing	Light speckled deer hair
Head	Brown dubbed fur or brown marabou

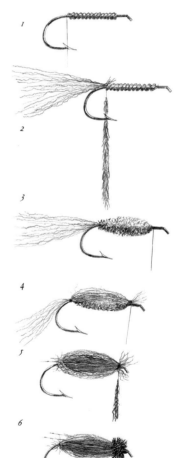

METHOD

Step 1 For the Deep Pupa pre-weight the hook with lead or copper wire, then take the thread down the shank. I always coat the lead and the thread with a little varnish, at this stage, as an anti-slip device. This prevents the lead and the subsequent dressing from turning around the hook.

Step 2 At the tail end tie in a bunch of Sparkle Yarn, already teased out. Onto the tying thread dub the fur Sparkle Yarn mixture.

Step 3 Take the fur-laden thread up the shank and form the body.

Step 4 Divide and separate the Sparkle Yarn and take half over the back so that it covers the back and half way down the sides.

Step 5 Repeat with the remaining Sparkle Yarn underneath the hook and up the sides so that the body is more or less covered by the yarn. At each side tie in a few fibres of lemon duck, and dub some fur or brown marabou onto the tying thread.

Step 6 Wind on the head and finish the fly as usual.

For the Emergent Pupa the progression of tying is the same up to Step 5. Then, instead of the lemon duck fibres, a sparse bunch of deer hair is tied in on the top of the hook to form a wing.

Just outside the town of Nova Gorica in Yugloslavia, close to the Italian frontier, is one of the finest seafood restaurants I have ever eaten in. 'What has this to do with sedge pupa?' you may well ask. The restaurant is run by the two brothers Gasparin, one of whom happens to be a very good fly fisherman and fly tier. (I shall give his adult sedge patterns later.) The following fly, a pupal pattern, is used to great effect on some of the rivers of the area, the Baca, the Idrica and, of course, the fabulous Soca.

The body of this pupa pattern uses a form of rubber. The nearest substitute I have found is a material supplied by Traun River Products. An alternative is the material used in the manufacture of paint rollers; a light foam plastic backing with a raised upper surface.

THE GASPARIN PUPA

DRESSING

Hook	Mustad 9672 sizes 8–12
Thread	Black or brown pre-waxed
Tail	Sparse, a few black cock hackle fibres
Body	Cream-coloured foam plastic or latex
Thorax	Peacock herl
Hackle	A few fibres of ginger or honey hackle

The pattern is straightforward and poses no difficulties in tying. Like most of the pupa patterns it can be pre-weighted.

Spain has a legacy of fly fishing and fly dressing as long as that of any other country. The manuscript of Juan de Bergera, dating back to around 1624, bears witness to this. This document lists the flies for the Province of Leon, along with tying instructions, for fishing the early months of the season. To this day feathers from the famed *coqs de Leon* are highly regarded and prized for their sharp, pristine and glass-like quality. They were used by Juan de Bergera for his spider-dressed flies, and are used today for both wet and dry patterns. The following pupa pattern was devised by Luis Antunez Jr of Madrid and is tied to represent the pupal stage of a micro-caddis. It is fished in the surface film, representing a pupa that has, for some reason or another, failed to hatch. The original pattern is green, but it can be tied up in the range of pupal colours, i.e., brown, black, cream, olive and perhaps amber.

THE FLOATING MICRO-PUPA

DRESSING

Hook	Mustad 9578a sizes 18–20, Partridge L3a sizes 16–20
Thread	Brown or olive pre-waxed
Body	Green seal's fur or substitute
Rib	Brown silk
Thorax	Brown seal's fur or substitute

As you can see the fly is extremely simple to tie.

The following two patterns are also the creations of Luis Antunez Jr. The first is a pupa tied to represent the Grannom (*Brachycentrus subnubilus*), a sedge which is as common in Spain as it is throughout most of Europe. The adult sedge from mountainous areas, both Alpine and sub-Alpine, tend to be very much darker than lowland species (McLachlan).

THE GRANNOM PUPA

DRESSING

The Grannom Pupa

Hook	Mustad 3904a size 12, Partridge G3a size 12
Thread	Brown pre-waxed
Body	Light brown polypropylene dubbing
Rib	Dark brown thread
Thorax	Reddish-brown polypropylene dubbing
Wings	Grey mallard wing slips

UCERO

Ucero

This pattern is in the LaFontaine style of air-bubbled emerging pupae.

DRESSING

Hook	Mustad 3904a sizes 10–12, Partridge G3a sizes 10–12
Thread	Red pre-waxed
Tail	Short tuft of polypropylene dubbing or Sparkle Yarn
Body	Cinnamon polypropylene or Sparkle Yarn dubbing
Rib	Brown thread
Hackle	Polypropylene yarn or Sparkle Yarn, tied in a collar so that it flares backwards
Head	Red

THE EMERGENT PUPA

DRESSING

Hook	Mustad 94840 size 8–10
Thread	Black or brown pre-waxed
Body	Brown Antron or similar yarn
Overbody	White antron
Hackle	Sparse grey mottled mallard breast sloping backwards with a few strands of metallic sparkle yarn. A small tuft of natural red hackle fibres on top of the hook
Thorax	Brown ostrich herl

Emergent Pupa

This pattern is tied in the same way as the La Fontaine sparkle pupae.

Sometimes, for various reasons, the pupa fails to release itself from the pupal skin and remains trapped in the surface film, where, of course, it often falls victim to the ever-hungry trout. This modern Austrian pattern by Roman Moser imitates this type of pupa well. It utilises the good floating properties of both natural deer hair and polyurethane foam.

MOSER'S FLOATING PUPA

DRESSING

Hook	Mustad 3904a or Partridge G3a sizes 10–14
Thread	Brown pre-waxed
Tail	Deer hair, grey or dyed brown
Body	Deer hair, grey or dyed brown
Head	Thin polyurethane foam

All over Europe a number of small nymph/pupa patterns are used for trout, but none more so than for the grey lady of the streams, the grayling. All of these patterns have at their head a small bead, sometimes gold, sometimes silver and sometimes of another colour. Although these flies are not strictly a pupa pattern, their shape and method of fishing lend themselves to the sedge pupa concept. These flies are to be found in France, Switzerland, Austria, Germany and Italy. Many are used to imitate anything from stonefly larvae to Ephemerid larvae, but as I have said they can be used very successfully during a rise to the hatching caddis. In fact, they suit the sink and draw method of retrieve very well indeed. The following three patterns were created by Francesco Palu of Udine in Italy.

Floating Sedge Pupa

THE GOLDEN PERLA

Golden Perla

DRESSING

Hook	Mustad 38930 sizes 12–16
Thread	Black or brown pre-waxed
Tail	None
Body	Peacock herl
Back	A strand of gold tinsel
Hackle	Sparse natural light red cock or hen
Head	Golden bead

LUCIFERO

Lucifero

DRESSING

Hook	Mustad 38930 sizes 14–16
Thread	Black or brown pre-waxed
Tail	A few ginger cock hackle fibres
Body	Bronze peacock herl
Hackle	Dark ginger cock or hen
Head	Pearl bead

DIABOLICA PERLA

Diabolica Perla

DRESSING

Hook	Mustad 38930 sizes 12–16
Thread	Black or brown pre-waxed
Tail	Dark blue dun cock hackle fibres (black will do)
Body	Orange wool or fur
Rib	Gold wire
Hackle	Dark blue dun cock or hen (black will do)
Head	Pearl bead

Just to prove the point, Roman Moser sent me a number of suitable pupal patterns. I have already given his floating pattern on page 63, but two other flies, which he considers to be essential for such rivers as the Traun, also make use of the bead head. The shiny brass not only provides weight for the fly but, by its very nature, the shine also proves attractive to both trout and the fabulous grayling found in that river of rivers.

The Gold-Headed Pupa

THE GOLD-HEADED PUPA (CLEAR WATER)

DRESSING

Hook	Partridge Sedge Hook sizes 8–10 (with barb flattened to make it barbless)
Thread	Brown pre-waxed
Body	Fluffy wool grey/brown
Head	Shiny brass bead

THE GOLD-HEADED PUPA (DARK WATER)

DRESSING

Hook	Partridge Sedge Hook sizes 8–10 (with barb flattened to make it barbless)
Thread	Brown pre-waxed
Body	Body gill or cream fur
Back	Spectraflash sheet
Rib	Copper wire
Hackle	Soft grey hackle
Head	Shiny brass bead

Gold-Headed Pupa

To complete this series of bead-head pupae, I would like to give an example of a Swiss pattern used for grayling. This fly comes from the Vallorbe area of Switzerland. A few years ago, after a visit to the magnificent caves of that area, I watched local fishermen test their skills on some equally magnificent grayling, using minute flies such as this pattern.

The Swiss Bead-Head Pupa

THE SWISS BEAD-HEAD PUPA

DRESSING

Hook	Mustad 3904A sizes 14–20
Thread	Black pre-waxed
Body	White plastic strip
Thorax	Dark brown feather fibre
Hackle	Wispy black hen hackle fibres below the hook with a few longer strands over the top like antennae
Head	Silver bead

Roman Moser sent me many other Austrian flies to imitate the pupal stage of the caddis, most of which are sold by Traun River Products of West Germany. The last of his pupa flies given here looks extremely attractive, for in the dubbing he combines chopped up Crystal Hair, a Mylar-type product normally used as a winging medium. This addition to the body medium causes it to scintillate in a most enticing manner.

THE GREY PUPA

DRESSING

Hook	Partridge Sedge Hook sizes 8–10
Thread	Brown pre-waxed
Body	Grey polypropylene dubbing mixed with silver Crystal Hair (use chopped-up Mylar or a similar product)
Head	Copper wire

The Guy Plas company of Marcilac-la-Croisille in the Limousin area of France, not far from the famous porcelain-manufacturing town of Limoges, produces a number of excellent flies. Like the flies from the other side of the Pyrenees in Spain, they tend to use the crystal-like hackles from specially bred cockerels, the *coqs de Leon* in Spain and the equally famous birds from the Limousin, an area where excellent cockerels are bred purely for their fly-dressing hackles. I was shown this pattern some years ago on a visit to a fishing club conclave in Spain.

PHRYGA-NYMPH

DRESSING

Hook	Mustad 3906b or VMC 8527 sizes 8–10 (it can be tied on long shank hooks also)
Thread	Yellow pre-waxed
Body	Tapered, a mixture of yellow and brown fur dubbing. (Other body colours can be tied, i.e., brown, green, black, cream, orange and olive)
Rib	Brown silk
Hackle	On the top of the hook only, ash-grey colour
Emergent wings	Brown and grey mottled spade feather fibres flanking the body

METHOD

Step 1   Wind the tying thread down the shank of the hook and tie in a length of brown silk for the rib. Dub the fur or wool mixture onto the tying thread.

Step 2   Wind the fur-laden thread up the hook, forming a robust tapered body. Follow this with even turns of the brown silk rib.

Step 3   On top of the hook tie a bunch of feather fibres taken from a

spade feather known as *indio acerado* (this is the Spanish nomenclature, see note).

Step 4 At the sides of the hook tie in bunches of feather fibre taken from a spade feather called *pardo flor de escoba*, this is a brown mottled feather with a touch of yellow (see note). Finish the fly in the usual way. The fly can be pre-weighted.

FLY DRESSING NOTE: COLOURS OF THE HACKLES OF THE *COQS DE LEON*

The famous Spanish cock hackles are divided into two types, the plain colours called *indio* and the mottled hackles termed *pardo*. We will come across these again in the chapter dealing with the adult sedge. I am told that there is something in the diet and also in the climate of the area in the province of Leon that dictates the quality of the hackles in these special cockerels. If they are moved to other areas of Spain they are reputed to lose some of the sheen and sparkle, and become decidedly lack lustre.

SOLID COLOURS (*INDIO*)

indio negrisco	black
indio rubion	natural red
indio plateado	silver grey
indio acerado	ash-grey
indio palometas	white
indio avellandado	brownish-grey
indio perla	pearl-grey

MOTTLED COLOURS (*PARDO*)

pardo flor de escoba	colour of the flower of the wild broom
pardo sarrioso	a mottled brown like the hair of the mountain chamois
pardo corzuno	Colour of the hair on a roebuck deer
pardo aconchado	a mottled brown as found on a brown conch shell

There are over 30 different mottled hackle varieties. One of the patterns given in the Juan de Bergera manuscript has been deemed a sedge pattern. In fact, its unique tying places it firmly in the sedge pupa format. It is a very similar fly to the modern Guy Plas pattern given above. It is classed as a 'Ninfa Leonesas'. The name given by Bergera for this fly was Salticas de San Juan. There were, in fact, three colour variations but I give only one here.

SALTICAS DE SAN JUAN

DRESSING

Hook	Mustad 94841 sizes 10–14
Thread	Yellow
Body	Pale yellow silk
Rib	Dark yellowy-orange
Thorax	Colour as rib
Side Hackle	*Indio plateado* (pearl-grey)
Head Hackle	*Flor de Escoba* (mottled brown/yellow)
Head	Yellow

The unique style of Spanish fly dressing is given in a later chapter (see pages 92–93).

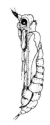

CHAPTER EIGHT

FISHING THE SEDGE PUPA

Darwell Reservoir lies in a gentle fold of the Sussex Downs, in the soft heartland of Southern England. Not many miles from this water, in the year 1066, the date imprinted on every schoolchild's mind, the Battle of Hastings took place. It was there that the flower of Saxon England fell beneath the iron-shod horses' hooves of the mail clad Norman knights. They had fought to the last man; a circle of house carls cut down around the body of their stricken king, their blood mingling with his and seeping into the chalky soil of Senlac. The victorious William, along with his half-brother, the warlike Bishop Odo of Bayeux, and a motley collection of Normans, Bretons, other Frenchmen, freebooters and mercenaries may well have ridden on the very ground which, centuries later, was flooded to provide a public reservoir. The prints of the horses' hooves are now etched in the memory of the Sussex clay; an invisible ghostly imprint in the soul of the land.

We arrived at the water on a day in late May. Thoughts of the Norman Conquest were furthest from our minds. To be perfectly honest, at the time we did not even appreciate that we might be treading on ground steeped in history, a place where possibly the discarded weapons of the fleeing English rusted to red powder beneath the sod. We were there to fish and I do not have to tell you what goes through a fly fisherman's mind at the start of a fishing day – not a lot, other than the hopes of a good day with plenty of fish. So we said no prayers for the unfortunate Harold, neither did we mentally sympathise with the sore fingers of the English nuns as they stitched the interminably long tapestry now ensconced in the Normandy town of Bayeux. The only thing on my mind was trout.

We crossed over the dam and settled down in a corner where the prevailing wind was kind, allowing us to cast across the direction of the breeze. The wind itself had obviously come, like the conquering

William, from across the Channel. It still held the tang of salt upon its breath. The area we were fishing held a few weed patches, and among these weedy areas there hatched a good number of Summer Duns. Trout cruised in close to the bank and every so often rose with an untidy splash. We hastily put on large olive dry flies, only for them to be totally ignored by the feeding fish. There was an obvious rise, and just as noticeable was the fact that the fish were ignoring both the natural Summer Duns and our hastily put on flies. I stopped fishing for a while, lit my pipe and watched the water. It was then that I saw it – a sedge fluttering among the water weed. That was it, they were taking sedges! I called out to my companions, whose success up until now was matching my own, and sedges were dutifully put on the end of the leader. Imagine our frustration as our roof-winged artificials were treated exactly the same as the olive dry flies.

I cannot remember who first put on the Amber Nymph, it may even have been me, but that was the fly that did the trick; we were all soon into fish. Up until then we had been doubly deceived. We were at first fooled into thinking that the trout were taking the floating duns and, secondly, after appreciating that we were witnessing a confused mixed hatch, we were hoodwinked into believing that the trout were rising to the adult sedge instead of the hatching pupae. Now, with experience, I have come to recognise the impetuous rise of a greedy pupae-chasing trout.

When a trout is feeding on pupae, it tends to throw a lot of its normal caution to the winds. It realises that the pupae are a nice meaty mouthful, the only threat to this feeding desire being the fairly rapid ascent of the pupae. The trout, in their eagerness to take such delicacies, follow the pupae as they rise from the bottom. The impetus of the chase often carries the trout through the surface in a welter of foam and water. It is not the deliberate sip sip of a trout mopping up surface food in a casual but studied manner; it is more of a hunting attack rather than a selective approach. Pupae feeding fish can hit your fly very hard indeed. The take can be of rod-snatching ferocity – it is as though the trout fear that their prey is about to escape. With their white maws open and fins a-bristle, they hit the pupae as though feeding was going out of fashion the following day.

Bewl Water lies right on the border of Kent and Sussex, a longish stone's throw from Darwell Reservoir. This is a comparatively new water, controlled by the South East Water Authority. It is perhaps the closest day-ticket water to my home and a water on which I have had some very good days' fishing over the last eight years. I remember on one occasion taking a boat out in early summer. I suppose it was late June for I was in shirt sleeves. I had gone right down an arm of the reservoir called Hook Straight, and throughout the morning fish came steadily to slowly fished lures. Around three o'clock a more pronounced rise commenced; once more it was the reliable sedge that was prompting this surface activity. This time there was no congratulatory shaking of hands as a dry sedge pattern was put on the leader, for I had by now come to recognise that the first sign of sedge activity is usually prompted by pupae-chasing trout. It is only later, as the light fades, that they change their tactics and search the surface for the hairy-legged adult sedge. Then their behaviour is a little more genteel, akin to ladies at a vicarage tea party and less like reckless, beserk Vikings hell bent on mayhem and destruction.

A well-tried Invicta wet fly was placed on the point, and two sedge pupae patterns were carefully tied on the droppers. I lifted the anchor and controlled the boat into a drift through the area of greatest activity. Fish were taken on all three flies; sometimes two at a time. One particular drift earned me a brown trout of about a $1\frac{1}{2}$ lb (680g) on the Invicta and a plump rainbow of equal weight on the top dropper. The brown trout wished to dive to the bottom and the rainbow wanted to leap out of the water, so in essence they fought each other and were duly netted. This method of fishing can be highly productive. There are those who will argue that the choice of flies would be better placed if the Invicta or a similar fly was on the top dropper and the pupa pattern on the point. Well, I would not argue with this at all but only say that that is how I had rigged my leader on that occasion.

The length of leader and correct positioning of the droppers can be quite critical, not because the fish will ignore the flies any other way, but for maximum effect in the working of the flies. The recommended leader length would be something in the order of 18 ft in length, with the top dropper or bob fly approximately 3 ft away from the join to the fly line. The second dropper, if you are going to fish one, should be about 6 ft from the point fly. For reservoir fishing, when the unexpected can happen, and a fish between 3-lb (1.36 kg) and double figures could take your fly, then a tippet strength of around 5 lb should be the minimum considered. Anything less and the false attitude of being sporting and fishing light results in a trophy fish snapping the leader and departing to depths unknown with your fly and a length of leader in its scissors. If this occurs it is not what I call sporting at all, it is not even bad luck, it is downright stupidity. The ones that get away are inevitably the big fish, and if the chances of catching one of these large trout is a possibility, then one should fish accordingly. It is not clever and certainly not sporting to allow a fish to escape with a barbed hook in its mouth, along with half your trailing leader. I am not saying that you will not get a broken line by using a 5-lb leader, but at least you are equalising the struggle a little and giving yourself a more than 50/50 chance of landing the fish. We do not go fishing to lose fish, we go to catch them.

Sometimes I am asked, 'What length do you have your droppers on the leader?' I have found a dropper of 6–7 in to be about right, but I must say there is a touch of hypocrisy about this reply, for in the heat of the fishing I usually nibble away at this length and find that I am quite often down to fishing a next-to-useless 2 or 3 in. Now, in an ideal world, one should, of course, tie on a new dropper in those circumstances, and this is exactly what you should do. I expect, however, like me, common sense, hand in hand with patience, usually flies out of the proverbial window and you ignore the obvious and continue willy-nilly, but at least you know what you *should* do.

Quite often one can read in fishing books that one should fish the pupa by the 'sink and draw' method. This expression is more or less self-descriptive and bears some relationship to how the natural pupa behaves. It is most important to work the fly, no matter what type, as close as possible to the normal behaviour of the natural creature it is imitating. If the insect, or whatever, moves through the water as slowly as a sloth on a pub crawl, then fish your artificial accordingly, with a slow figure-eight retrieve. If it crawls along the bottom with no desire to venture into the main body of the water, then that is where you fish your fly, down where the action is likely to be. If, on the other hand, the natural insect is zipping through its environment at a rate of knots, then fast retrieving is the order of the day. In the case of the hatching sedge pupa, we know that the creature ascends from the bottom, usually quite quickly, to reach the surface. Accordingly, we should cast our flies out, allow them to sink, then retrieve in long steady pulls. That is basically what 'sink and draw' means; an emulation of a pupa rising to the surface.

So far, using the above examples, we have looked at the basic methods I adopt to fish the pupae in a given set of circumstances on stillwater. On stillwater the angler has control of the fly by his retrieve. On rivers some of this direct control is inevitably surrendered to the flow of the river and the vagaries of the currents, so a slightly different approach is necessary. The fisherman must learn to use these natural water movements to his advantage.

The River Exe, in the county of Devon, winds itself through some very lush and verdant farmland. However, it starts its life on windswept Exmoor, a place of winds and mists, sphagnum moss and bog cotton, where the buzzard glides high in the sky and the raven tumbles from the clouds. This is place, like its sister moor, Dartmoor, of mystery, a land where time has stood still, a place where lumps of granite point accusingly with phallic stone fingers at leaden rain-streaked skies.

I have fished the Exe for almost twenty years and have come to know some of its secrets and some of its whims. I now know where the dipper bobs to the majesty of clean water and dives to take the caddis. I know where trout lie to be comfortable and have a steady stream of food brought to them, or at least where they should lie. I have often taken a decent fish from a holding spot and come back the next time to find that another fish has taken up residence. This is river logic; a good feeding station is always a good feeding station. The trout realise this and if a good lie becomes vacant then another fish will soon move in. The only thing that will alter this natural event could be the floods of the winter months. These can be quite a common occurrence, swiftly changing a mild even-tempered stream into a raging torrent. These floods can thus alter the topography of the river and wipe out many previous fish-holding lies. However, new ones are also formed, both feeding stations and those hideaway places that the trout consider to be their safety bolt holes. It is only a question of observation to find out where these new places are.

Time spent just looking at the river is never wasted. It is an essential part of river-craft. An hour spent watching the stream will serve you better than just casting a fly casually into the river in the hopes that some invisible fish will fall for the bait. There is one particular spot on the river I know well. I call it the Quarry Pool Run Off. At this pool the river takes an almost 90-degree turn. It swirls, a little confused, round the angles of the pool before tumbling out down the run off, as though relieved it has once more found its way. On one visit a sedge or two fluttered weakly in the bushes close to the river, but there was no evidence of a rise on the water. It was perhaps a little early so I decided to fish a small weighted sedge pupa.

Common sense tells you that in moving water, like a river or stream, anything moving from the bottom to the top is not going to rise vertically in the water. The currents are going to transport the creatures some distance from the place where they left their pupal cases. Some species actually rely on this current transference before hatching. They do not struggle to emerge as quickly as possible, but

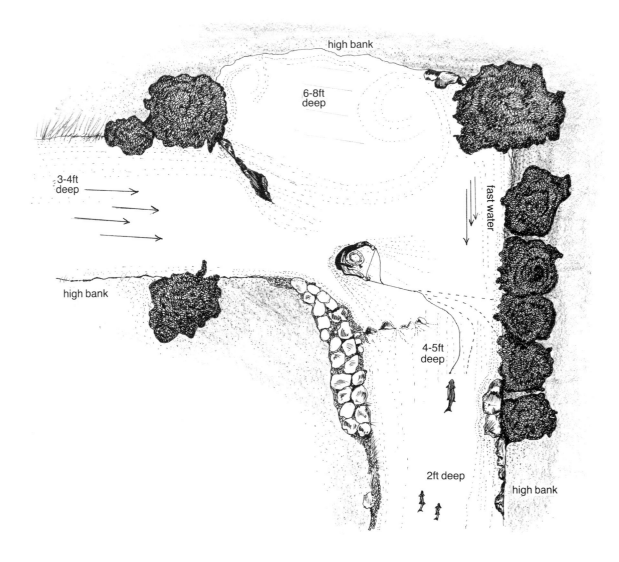

high bank

6-8ft
deep

3-4ft
deep

fast water

high bank

4-5ft
deep

2ft deep

high bank

Quarry Pool

drift in the water for some considerable distance before emerging through the surface film. As you can see from the diagram of the pool, there are two ways of fishing this particular run off pool: upstream from the left-hand bank, or downstream from the same bank. Bushes and a high bank prevent any real approach from the right-hand bank. Past experience has shown me that, in the case of this particular small pool, an upstream approach tends to disturb the fish more than the downstream cast. The shallower water and exposed bank tend to send small fish scurrying into the deeper water of the small pool. These fish, in turn, then seem to set up an anxiety syndrome in the fish already resident in the pool, and then one's flies are more often than not ignored.

I carefully stepped into the water on the edge of the Quarry Pool and cast the pupa into the fast water as it sped out of the pool along the right-hand bank. My line curved out with the fastness of the flow, but by mending the line my fly curved out of the fast water and dropped over the lip into the small pool. The take was like greased lightning. One moment my fly was curling into the pool, the next it was screaming down the river. The fish turned out to be a grayling of about $1\frac{1}{4}$ lb (567 g). I rested the pool for about half an hour and did the same thing again, casting from exactly the same spot with exactly the same fly. This time the take was even quicker and after a short fight a brown of the same weight lay on the bank.

The last time I fished that spot my fly was taken by a brown trout of very large proportions (of course, I mean large by the Exe's standards). I estimated it to have been about 3 lb (1.36 kg). I only saw its flank before the hook pulled out. About an hour later that evening the fish were rising the length of the stream to small adult sedges; the time of the pupa was over.

On rivers, I tend to use a much smaller leader (9–10 ft maximum) than on stillwater, for obvious reasons. Long leaders are extremely difficult to control on the rivers that I fish, especially with weighted flies and the vagaries of the prevailing winds and, of course, where a degree of accurate presentation is very important. I concede that it may well be my lack of skill, but I feel more comfortable with the shorter leader. Again, on streams and rivers I only fish with one weighted fly and no droppers. The only time I use more than one fly on the leader is when I am fishing unweighted traditional spider-dressed wet flies.

On some rivers, of course, the use of more than one fly on a leader is forbidden. The River Krka in Slovenia is such a river. It is a river of sawmills and sedges, a river with long slow glides, fast, stepped weirs and, where the water leaves these old mills, a veritable hurly burly of white foam. I love the fishing in that particular republic of Yugoslavia; the fly life found on its streams is as thronged as it is varied. Some waters explode with large hatches of mayflies – so many that the very air above the rivers seems squeezed out by their numbers. On the limestone crystal rivers that tumble out of the Julian Alps, stoneflies flutter above the fast moving streams like insectivorous confetti. On the River Krka it is the sedges that cause the fish to rise from the clear water depths.

It was late May when I last visited this river. Small Silver Sedges (*Lepistoma hirtum*) were on the water along with some larger sedges, like the Large Cinnamon (*Potamophylax latipennis*) and the Grey Sedge (*Odontocerum albicorne*). They were fluttering above the stream and every so often they would descend to the surface in skipping flight. I assumed they were ovipositing. In the bankside vegetation other sedges shunned the daylight; among these I recognised the Black Sedge (*Athripsodes nigronervosus*), hiding amidst the grass root jungle.

For two days I had steadily taken fish on a variety of dry sedge patterns, all of them large flies. My good friend Dr Voljč of Ljubljana had tied some specials for me which proved very attractive. I also used some deer-hair patterns of my own as well as some sedges kindly sent to me by Roman Moser from Austria. All caught their fair share of fish. On the third day just as many sedges were on the water, but try as I could not one fish did I rise. I watched the water carefully and realised that the fish were no longer taking the ovipositing females, but were more concerned with a new hatch of sedge. They were feeding avidly on the emerging pupa. Some good fish were rising further up the bank, but trees and bushes prevented me from presenting the pupae to this feeding zone. Every time I tried to extend my cast upstream and give it that little bit of extra distance to reach these fish, I caught the bushes and more often than not lost my fly.

On this third day the water had dropped and this enabled me to cross the river and tackle these fish from a more convenient angle, downstream rather than up as I had being doing. I put on a Brown Sedge pupa and cast across the river. By mending the line, I managed to drift my pupa into the active feeding area. Just as the line reached where I thought the fish to be, I raised the rod so that my pupa would rise upwards in the water. (This is a cross between the Leisering lift method and the traditional, induced-take method practised so well by the likes of Frank Sawyer and Oliver Kite.) I had obviously done the right thing for I was rewarded with two trout from this spot, a brown of just over a pound and a fat rainbow which tipped the scales at 2½ lb (1.13 kg).

This particular stretch of the river was more suited to the dry fly. The river glides for just over 500 yd through meadows. Although it flows with deceptive swiftness, it is smooth and ripple free. Other parts of the river are quite different. In about 3 miles there are three working timber mills, complete with water races that gush water so fast that you cannot stand in the flow. It was close to one of these mills, where the main current sped along the opposite bank and the

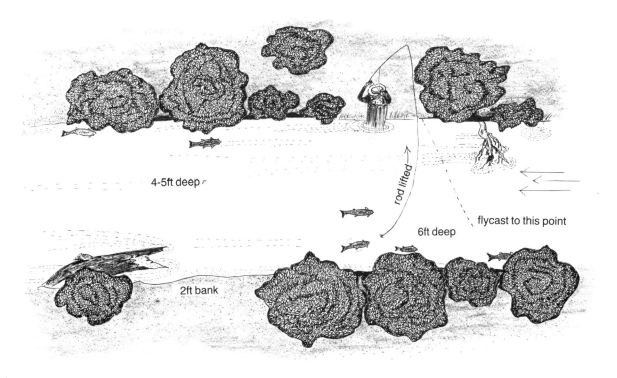

4-5ft deep

rod lifted →

flycast to this point

6ft deep

2ft bank

Slow stretch of the Krka River

trees overhung the river, shading any waiting trout, that I cast my first fly on the Krka. There was a slight chill in the air after the sun had gone down, and I shivered as the water lapped under my armpits. Because of the sudden drop in temperature that evening, there was no great sedge activity. There was barely a discernible rise so I chose to fish a pupa pattern I had made from hare's fur. In fact, it was basically an overgrown Gold Ribbed Hare's Ear but in a distinct sedge pupa shape. I cast this somewhat overweighted fly up and across to the opposite bank and frantically mended my line in order to keep the fly running in the fast water beneath the tree overhang. It was a speculative cast into a spot where I thought a trout might be. Call it speculation if you like, or Welsh luck maybe, although if you are generous you may call it skill, for the fly had not travelled more than a few yards when a hard take jerked the rod in my hand. After a spirited fight I managed to land a 3-lb (1.36 kg) wild rainbow with a tail as perfect as a Chinese fan. An autopsy on the stomach contents revealed a number of Brown Sedge pupae, thus vindicating my choice of fly. It is always satisfying when this sort of confirmation happens. You give yourself a mental pat on the back and your face usually bears a somewhat smug grin.

The three methods adopted in the examples given are all basically the same but with subtle differences forced upon me by the lie of the trout and the topography of the rivers. All three approaches were across and down in their initial cast direction, but it is the final stages that differed. On the Exe I used the flow of water in that pool run off to swing my fly into the spot exactly where the fish were. Careful control and mending of the line ensured that my fly did not overshoot and start to rise behind the fish or come to the surface with drag before it reached the fish.

The second example was an indication that an approach from a more convenient position is often more successful than continually trying to achieve the near impossible. By crossing the river and once more casting across the stream, I was able to take the fish by physically raising the rod high in order to make the fly look like a pupa about to break the surface.

The third example was to use the fast flow of the water and, by a constant mending of the line, allow the fly to travel at the same speed as the water just below the surface, without drag, in just the way a natural creature would behave as it was being swept away in the turbulence before reaching more tranquil waters to hatch out.

Upstream methods can be successful if care is observed in not lining the fish. To do this, practise casting a left- or right-hand loop in the leader. This allows the fly to come down to the trout with the minimum of drag. Casting up and across into a fast flow requires that the rod be held fairly high and swept from right to left as the line becomes level with the angler. Direct downstream fishing needs a little care for the river takes over very quickly and your fly is dragged upwards very unnaturally. To prevent this, feed a little line through the rings manually, but the further away you are from the fish the more difficult it is to set the hook. The tendency is to pull the fly straight out of the fish's mouth.

Methods adopted for fishing caddis larvae still hold good for the pupae, especially for those sedge species whose pupae drift close to the bottom for some way before venturing further up into the water prior to hatching. I think perhaps the best approach to fishing, whether it be with pupae or larvae, and come to think of it the adult fly as well, is flexibility. Fish as the given circumstances dictate. If it is easier to fish upstream to a particular trout then that is what you should do. If you are forced to reach a trout by a downstream approach, then follow your judgement and fish downstream. Sometimes it is prudent to fish from the bank; on other occasions it is necessary to wade chest deep to approach your quarry. All the words written on a printed page will not catch you your trout. It is up to you and the fly on the end of your leader. How and where you put the fly is the essence of our sport, and this is dictated by the living water and the lie of the wary trout.

CHAPTER NINE

TYING THE ADULT SEDGE

A SEARCH FOR THE ANGLER'S SEDGE

Despite the apparent neglect of the sedge by past fly fishermen, there are still a large number of sedge patterns to be found in the archives of fly fishing. Over the centuries appreciation of the sedge as a potential weapon in the armoury of the fly fisherman appears to have had a somewhat muted acceptance. Why this should be remains something of a mystery. Was it because the mayflies were more evident in daylight hours and appeared to be on the water more than the sedge? Perhaps an answer can be found in the works of the angling writers themselves. Many of the books considered important were either written by men who concerned themselves with the verdant chalk streams where the mayfly was and still is king, or by erudite North Countrymen whose type of fly and style of fishing apparently had nothing to do with the sedge at all but with magical spider-dressed wet flies, although it is possible to interpret some of these as possible sedges. So where are we to find the sedge in any sort of numbers to satisfy what we now consider its justified importance? We do not have to look far, for our elusive sedge flies are to be found in the fly wallets of those anglers that fished the lakes of the British Isles. It is on such waters that the sedge is to be found, heavily disguised, in many of our traditional wet patterns. I am not only referring to the named sedge flies like the traditional Flags, Rails and Peters of Ireland, but to such classic wet flies as the Mallard series, Teal series, Grouse series, Woodcock series and other individual flies, many of them still in common use today. It is here that we find our missing historical sedge. Now whether the users of such flies considered them to be imitations of the family Trichoptera is another matter, but there is no doubt at all in my mind that that is how the trout view many of these flies, either as pupae or as adults. So if we fish the Mallard and Claret, Teal and Green, Grouse and

Yellow, etc., we are, in essence, fishing the wet sedge. There are many other flies in the fly wallets of the stillwater angler, which fit the sedge category: the Cinnamon and Gold, the Fiery Brown, the Invicta, the Silver Invicta and perhaps even the orange-coloured Dunkeld.

To find our first British sedge patterns, we must go back to the year 1496 and the 'Treatyse of Fysshynge with an Angle' from the *Boke of St Albans* produced by Dame Juliana Berners. Whether or not she wrote the book at all is not in debate here, but for the month of June we are given a fly called the 'Dun Cut'. This fly had a black body with sides of yellow and wings of buzzard bound with hemp. General consensus states that this is some form of sedge. Likewise for the month of July we are offered another fly called the 'Shell Fly'. This is a pattern with a green wool body, possibly ribbed with peacock herl, and again a wing of buzzard feather. Short of being able to identify this pattern as any other form of insect, we can assume that this, too, could be a sedge of some sort.

Dun Cut

Shell Fly

The next book of importance to the fly fisherman was the *Art of Angling* written by Thomas Barker in 1651. Apart from giving details on fly dressing, most of his patterns were general flies, many of the 'palmer' variety, and as far as can be interpreted none appears to be an actual sedge.

The year 1676 gives us the Charles Cotton contribution to Izaak Walton's *The Compleat Angler*. In his list of about 65 artificial fly patterns a number of sedges are to be found. Apart from one or two 'brown' flies in March and April, one of which could possibly be a sedge (the Grannom?), we have the same 'Dun Cut' of the 'Treatyse' appearing in May, but Cotton's fly is given two horns at the head, made from squirrel hair, these antennae possibly confirming its sedge status. Also in May there is a fly referred to as the 'Camlet' fly. Could this be a sedge? Possibly, for he refers to it as being shaped like a moth.

For the month of June, Cotton gives a pattern called the 'Barm Fly'. Although he calls it a dun it would seem that all sorts of flies were referred to as duns for about 200 years after Cotton, so that 'dun' did not mean, as it does now, the sub-imago of the Ephemeroptera. (In the nineteenth century Francis Francis also gives a 'Barm Fly' and, furthermore, he specifically calls it *Phryganidae*.) The 'Barm Fly' gets its name from its yeasty colour. The body was tied with the yellowish fur from a dun-coloured cat and the wing was grey mallard. In July we also have once more the 'Shell Fly', but in Cotton's opinion we have here a fly to imitate a sawfly larva of some sort, for unlike Dame Juliana's pattern it has no wing, and Cotton seems to think it falls out of willow bushes onto the water. Could his 'Camel-Brown' fly of September be a sedge, along with his other selection for that month, a fly tied with the dark hair of a badger's skin mixed with the yellow down of a sandy-coloured hog?

The first true identification of anglers' sedges is to be found in James Chetham's book of 1681, *The Angler's Vade Mecum*. For the month of March we have a reference to the 'Greentail', the old name for the Grannom (*Brachycentrus subnubilus*). The fly was made from the hair of a brown spaniel's ear, but emphasis was put on the tail end, which was made from sea-green wool. The wings came from a shepstare (starling).

The Art of Angling was published in 1747 by father and son, Richard and Charles Bowlker of Ludlow in the county of Shropshire. In this book two definite sedge patterns are given. For the month of April we find once more the 'Green Tail' but now it is also called the 'Granam'. They tied the fly from a hare's mask and the wing from a partridge or pheasant quill. For June we are given the 'Cadis Fly'. They even give the fact that the four-winged fly is born from the 'cod bait', another old name for the caddis larva. This pattern of theirs is a buff-coloured fly with a body of buff mohair, wings of a buff hen and a pale yellow cock hackle.

The nineteenth century gave the world of angling literature a veritable wealth of books, too many to deal with here in any detail, but mention must be made of one or two whose contribution to the world of the artificial fly is considered to be significant. How could we not mention Alfred Ronald's book, published in 1836, and called *The Fly Fisher's Entomology*. This contains a wealth of artificial patterns and details of the time of the season to fish them. Among his flies are the following sedges: the Sand Fly, the Grannom, the Silverhorns and the Cinnamon Fly.

In the north of England we have the great writer T. E. Pritt. His book was first published in 1885 as *Yorkshire Trout Flies* and republished as *North Country Trout Flies* in 1886. Among his many patterns we once more find the Greentail, the Sand Fly and the Cinnamon. It is also possible that the Red and Brown Owl flies could be sedge flies and perhaps even the Sandy Moorgame.

What patterns did F. M. Halford give in his book *Floating Flies and How to Dress Them*, published in 1886? We actually have a larval pattern for the Grannom, the Adult Grannom, the Silver Sedge, the Orange Sedge and a Dark Sedge. There is also the Welshman's Button.

In Spain, in the year 1624, the *Manuscrito de Astorga* was published by Juan de Bergera, 29 years before the *Compleat Angler* of Izaak

Walton. Mention has already been made of the feathers used in these Spanish flies in Chapter 7. A number of de Bergera's flies have been interpreted as sedges. The other major work to come from Spain is the manuscript, by Luis Pena de Leon in 1825, which is an update of the *Manuscrito de Astorga*. Although the patterns are traditional spider flies of that area of Spain, some are thought to be wet sedge imitations. The dressing of some of these classic Spanish wet flies is given later along with the distinct method of their tying.

THE WET SEDGE

Although wet fly imitations are used on rivers it is on still water that they come into their own. As mentioned earlier, many of our traditional lake flies could be interpreted as sedge flies of one species or another. The dressings of such flies are to be found in most books on fly dressing, so I feel there is no great need to include them here. Instead, I will endeavour to give the dressings of those flies that are specifically intended to represent a sedge, flies such as some of the patterns used sub-surface on the Irish loughs; patterns like the Rails, Flags and Peters, all of which are wet flies but can also be tied as dry patterns if the fancy takes you.

The first fly we are going to consider is a pattern that not only has stood the test of time, but continues to catch fish for many anglers at home and abroad. I refer to the Invicta and its second cousin the Silver Invicta. During a sedge rise, especially on stillwater, this pattern is highly effective. It may well be that the trout view this pattern as a hatching sedge pupa or even as an imitation of those female sedges that go underwater to lay their eggs.

Invicta

THE INVICTA

DRESSING

Hook	Mustad Limerick 3123 sizes 6–12
Thread	Yellow or black pre-waxed
Tail	Golden pheasant crest
Body	Yellow seal's fur or substitute
Rib	Oval gold tinsel
Hackle	Light natural red, palmered, and jay or dyed blue guinea fowl at the throat
Wing	Hen pheasant centre tail

James Ogden is credited with creating the classic Invicta fly. The Silver Invicta or the Silver Knicker as it sometimes known, especially in Wales, was devised by John Eastwood. I have found this silver version to be highly effective on some rivers and on analysing its success for me, I realised I always used it late in the afternoon at a time when some species of sedge start to appear. Without doubt the trout take this fly for a hatching sedge complete with its silvery air bubble. This silver variant differs from the original in the body which, in this case, is flat silver tinsel ribbed with silver oval, and generally does not have a body hackle.

The Red Tailed Invicta, invented by Richard Walker, is the same as the original fly but with a bright red tail. The other variants are tied in the same way as the original Invicta, except that the body and hackles are of a different colour. They are as follows:

The Orange Invicta   Orange body and orange palmer hackle
The Olive Invicta   Olive body and olive palmer hackle
The Black Invicta   Black body and black palmer hackle
The Green Invicta   Green body and green palmer hackle

The next sedge we are going to look at is an Irish pattern that has crossed the Irish Sea and become a firm favourite with reservoir anglers all over the British Isles. I refer to the fly Green Peter. Some maintain that this pattern imitates the natural sedge *Phryganea varia*, but the only thing wrong with this assumption is that body colour of the natural is an overall black, while the fly is usually called the Speckled Peter. Having said that, I do not think it matters greatly as the trout view this fly with great favour.

THE GREEN PETER

DRESSING

Hook   Mustad 94841 or 3123 size 10
Thread   Green pre-waxed
Body   Pea-green seal's fur
Rib   Fine oval gold tinsel
Hackle   Ginger Hen
Wing   Grey pheasant wing

For the dry version, substitute with ginger palmered cock hackle and a barred hen pheasant wing.

The next fly is a pattern tied to imitate the closely allied species *Phryganea obsoleta*, known as the Peter or Dark Peter.

Plate 1   CADDIS LARVAE

Stick Fly   Twig Caddis   Pebble Caddis

Latex Larva   Latex Larva   Breadcrust

Strawman Nymph   Sand Caddis   Hare Caddis

Walker Caddis   Horn Caddis   Green Stick Fly

Hydropsyche   Hydropsyche (No. 2)   Plant Case Caddis

Plate 2 SEDGE PUPAE

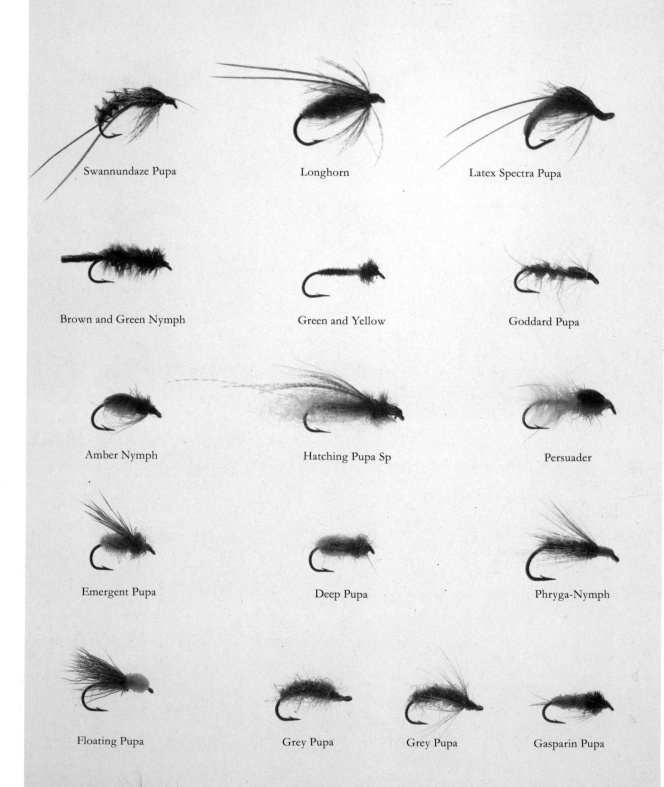

Swannundaze Pupa

Longhorn

Latex Spectra Pupa

Brown and Green Nymph

Green and Yellow

Goddard Pupa

Amber Nymph

Hatching Pupa Sp

Persuader

Emergent Pupa

Deep Pupa

Phryga-Nymph

Floating Pupa

Grey Pupa

Grey Pupa

Gasparin Pupa

Plate 3 MOSTLY WET

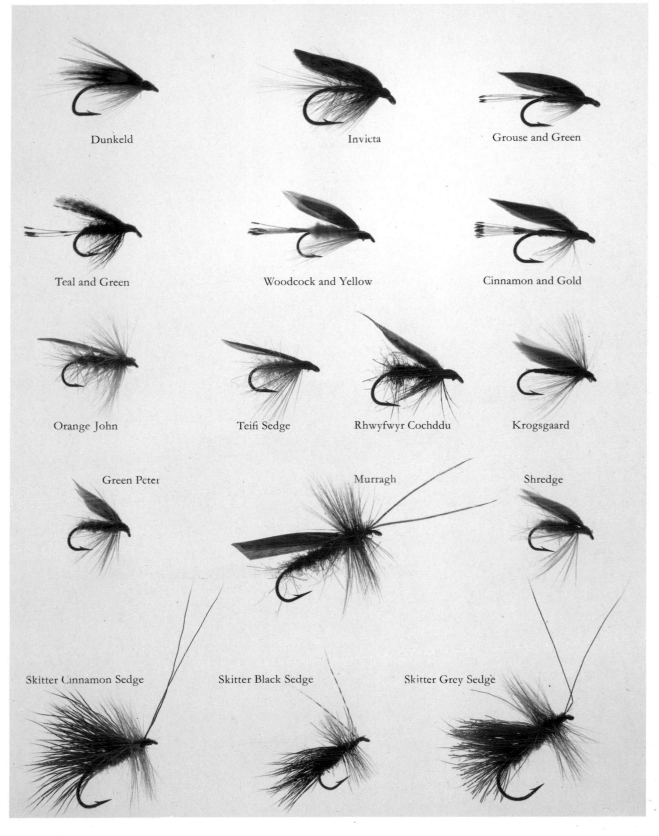

Dunkeld

Invicta

Grouse and Green

Teal and Green

Woodcock and Yellow

Cinnamon and Gold

Orange John

Teifi Sedge

Rhwyfwyr Cochddu

Krogsgaard

Green Peter

Murragh

Shredge

Skitter Cinnamon Sedge

Skitter Black Sedge

Skitter Grey Sedge

Plate 4   BRITISH AND AMERICAN SEDGE PATTERNS

Walker's Red Sedge

G&H Sedge

Cinnamon Sedge

Caperer

Light Sedge Thomas

Dark Sedge Thomas

Lane's Cinnamon Sedge

Henryville

King River

Elk Hair Caddis

Brown Micro   Grey Micro   Black Micro

Delta

Dancing Caddis Ginger

Dancing Caddis
(Brown and Yellow)

Dancing Caddis
(Brown and Green)

Plate 5   EUROPEAN SEDGES

Moser Sedge (Austria)   Moser Cinnamon (Austria)   Light Sedge (Rubel Bavaria)   Dark Sedge (Rubel Bavaria)

Light Sedge (Rocher French)   Cul Sedge (Devaux French)   Dark Sedge (Rocher French)   Partridge Sedge (French)

Palu's Mottled Sedge (Italian)   Palu's Red Sedge (Italian)   Black Sedge (Spanish)   Sarriosa (Spanish)

Karsten's Mottled Sedge (Denmark)   Karsten's Brown Sedge   Karsten's Cream Sedge   Poly Sedge (Denmark)

Fratnik's Grey Sedge (Yugoslavia)   Fratnik's Brown Sedge   Foxtail Sedge (No. 1)   Foxtail Sedge (No. 2)

Voljč Grouse Wing   Voljč Silver Sedge   Voljč Caperer   Voljč Black Sedge (Yugoslavia)

Plate 6

1 Caddis Cases

2 Caddis Case, *Limnephilus rhombicus*

3 Caddis Case, *Limnephilus politus*

4 Caddis Case, *Triaenodes bicolor*

5 Lava, *Rhyacophila dorsalis*

6 Lava, *Hydropsyche sp*

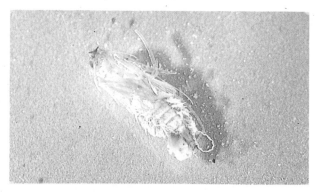

7 Sedge Pupa

8 The Black Silverhorn, *Mystacides azurea*

Plate 7

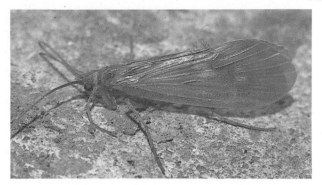

9   The Brown Sedge, *Anabolia nervosa*

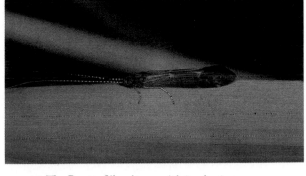

10   The Brown Silverhorn, *Athripsodes cinereus*

11   The Brown Silverhorn, *Athripsodes albifrons*

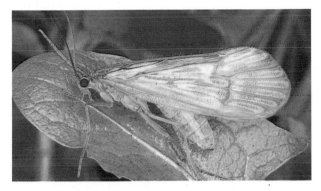

12   The Caperer, *Halesus digitatus*

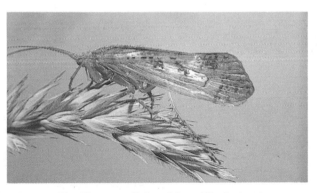

13   The Cinnamon Sedge, *Limnephilus flavicornis*

14   The Cinnamon Sedge, *Limnephilus lunatus*

15   The Dark Sedge, *Polycentropus flavomaculatus*

16   The Grannom or Greentail, *Brachycentrus subnubilus*

Plate 8

17 The Grouse Wing, *Mystacides longicornis*

18 Lane's Mottled Sedge, *Limnephilus marmoratus*

19 The Large Cinnamon Sedge, *Potamophylax latipennis*

20 The Mottled Sedge, *Glyphotaelius pellucidus*

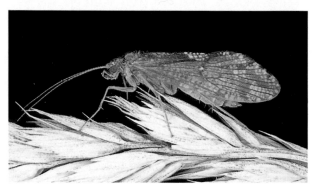

21 Ronald's Sand Fly, The Sand Fly, *Rhyacophila dorsalis*

22 The Silver or Grey Sedge, *Odontocerum albicorne*

23 The Small Red Sedge, *Tinodes waeneri*

24 The Yellow Spotted Sedge, *Philopotamus montanus*

THE DARK PETER

DRESSING

Hook	Mustad 94641 or 3123 sizes 8–12
Thread	Black pre-waxed
Body	Black or very dark green seal's fur
Rib	Fine oval gold tinsel
Hackle	Furnace hen hackle (palmered cock for dry version)
Wing	Dark speckled pheasant

There is also a fly called the Blue Peter. Being coloured, as it is, with dark blue seal's fur, places it somewhat into the fancy fly category, but who knows how the trout view it. Most, I suppose, accept it as a sedge.

Before we leave the Emerald Isle, mention must be made of the group of traditional sedge flies known as the Rails. They obtained this name from the material used for the wing. This came from the landrail or corncrake, which is, of course, a protected bird. E. J. Malone, in his excellent book *Irish Trout and Salmon Flies*, suggests using jay or golden pheasant wing feathers as an acceptable substitute. Some of the colours used for the bodies of these flies are black, brown, grey, claret, red and yellow. Many of these flies are also given a tail, often of golden pheasant tippet or sometimes brown mallard fibres. The dressing I give is for the Cinnamon Rail, a fair representation of the Cinnamon Sedge (*Limnephilus lunatus*).

THE CINNAMON RAIL

DRESSING

Hook	Mustad 3123 Limerick sizes 8–12
Thread	Brown pre-waxed
Tail	None in this rail pattern
Body	Cinnamon seal's fur
Rib	Fine oval gold or silver
Hackle	Dark ginger (hen for wet fly, cock for dry)
Wings	Landrail substitute

A modern British wet sedge, used on the large manmade waters of Rutland and Grafham, is a pattern called the Shredge. This fly was devised by Tony Knight as a combined shrimp and sedge imitation (a bit like crossing a donkey with an elephant to my mind). Steve Parton, the still-water boat expert, ties a version with dark sienna seal fur for the body. But to show you there is seldom such a thing as a new fly in fly dressing, I will also give the dressing for an Irish sedge of long standing that is more than similar to Knight's Shredge and Parton's Emerging Tobacco Sedge. I refer to the traditional series of sedges from Ireland called the Bann Sedges and to the Large Bann Sedge in particular. It may be a dry pattern, but to my mind, it is by coincidence, a very similar fly, as is the Cinnamon Rail already given.

Shredge

THE SHREDGE

DRESSING

Hook	Mustad 79672 or Partridge Sedge Hook sizes 10–12
Thread	Primrose pre-waxed
Body	Tobacco-coloured seal's fur
Rib	Fine gold wire
Hackle	Pale ginger hen
Wing	Grey mallard flight feathers

THE LARGE BANN SEDGE

DRESSING

Hook	Mustad 94841 sizes 8–10
Thread	Light brown pre-waxed
Body	Tobacco-coloured seal's fur
Rib	Fine oval gold
Hackle	Pale ginger (hen for wet, cock for dry)
Wing	Inner mallard flight feathers (sometimes dyed the same colour as the body)

The land of my birth is justly noted for many things, such as mountains and rivers, coal mines and steel (in the old days), choirs and chapel and, of course, rugby football, which is a religion in itself complete with the hymn-singing – when Wales are winning that is! Wales has always had a great number of fly tiers who tied flies for salmon, sewin (sea-trout) and, of course, the slim brown trout of rivers and llyns. Many of the flies have a pedigree going back almost 200 years or so. For many years my uncle had a fishing tackle shop in my home town of Barmouth, in the county of Merioneth (now Gwynedd) from where he sold a wide number of local patterns, many of which are unobtainable these days. Welsh flies had a character all of their own. Rough and ready many of them were, but it says something for their effectiveness that a large number are still in use today.

Perhaps one of the best books to come out of Wales in recent years was written by my good friend Moc Morgan and called *Fly Patterns for the Rivers and Lakes of Wales*. I use this book often to cure what all ex-patriot Welshmen suffer from; a sort of longing for the homeland which we call *Hiraeth*. It is the Celtic equivalent of the US 'homesick blues'! In this book there is a wealth of fly patterns for the principality and it is pleasing to note that the sedge was not ignored by the old-time fly fishermen of my country. The following four flies are Welsh sedge flies, fished by the traditional wet fly methods.

The first of the sedge flies was one called in Welsh *Rhwyfwyr mawr cochddu*. Roughly translated this means the big red/black sedge, a fly from the small town of Festiniog in North Wales. Here slate was quarried to roof fine buildings all over the world, and it is here that I played football as a schoolboy and where before me, my father and his brother also played for the town of Blaenau Festiniog in the 1920s. This fly was used as a dusk fly on the local lakes by the quarrymen anglers. It was usually fished as a top dropper or bob fly in a team of wet flies.

RHWYFWYR MAWR COCHDDU

DRESSING

Hook	Mustad 94840 size 8
Thread	Black
Body	Hair taken from the scrotum of a black ram (I would use some sort of substitute if I were you, seal's fur perhaps!)
Rib	Fine gold wire
Hackle	Brown partridge
Wing	Partridge tail flanked by brown owl

On smaller sizes it was called *Rhwyfwyr Bach Cochddu* and usually fished on size 12 hooks, but the dressing was exactly the same. For those of you who do not know, one of the traditional sheep breeds in Wales is the Welsh Black, hence all this talk of hair from a black ram's scrotum. There used to be a small flock of these sheep just outside Dolgellau. I would see them as I passed their field on my way from London to Barmouth to visit my family. They seemed to view me as one of their own! It takes one to know one I suppose.

The next sedge is the Green Ringed Sedge, called in Welsh *Rhwyfwyr Clychau Gwyrdd*. You will have gathered by now that the word *rhwyfwyr* means sedge.

RHWYFWYR CLYCHAU GWYRDD

Rhwyfwyr Clychau Gwyrdd

DRESSING

Hook	Mustad 94840 size 10
Thread	Green
Body	Hair from a black ram's scrotum (or substitute)
Rib	Green silk
Hackle	Brown partridge
Wing	Light coloured brown owl

Moc Morgan gives us another pattern from his own home locality in mid-Wales. This is a fly for the Teifi pools, a series of lakes high in the Teifi Valley, the last refuge of the red kite in the British Isles.

THE TEIFI POOLS SEDGE

DRESSING

Hook	Mustad 94840 sizes 10–12
Thread	Brown
Body	Orange wool or seal's fur
Rib	None given but I suspect that a gold wire rib could well have been used
Hackle	Dark ginger
Wing	Light dun hen wing quill slips

Wet sedge patterns are used extensively by many of the modern anglers who fish the large reservoirs, especially those who enjoy the match fishing aspect of fly fishing. Certainly the Green Peter came to the notice of more anglers because of the Irish international fly-fishing team. The rules laid down for fishing these events encourage the use of traditional-style flies. John Ketley once English team in these four-way internationals. The next fly is one of his.

ORANGE JOHN

DRESSING

Hook	Partridge Captain Hamilton wet fly size 10
Thread	Orange pre-waxed
Body	Orange seal's fur
Rib	Gold Goldfingering (a proprietary gold-coloured, met-allic embroidery thread)
Hackles	Palmered light brown honey hackle in the front
Wing	Hen pheasant, tied flat on top of the hook

It would be a little strange, if not churlish, if I did not give a mention to those sedge patterns that are to be found over the border in Scotland. As stated earlier, many of the traditional 'loch' wet flies can possibly be classed as sedge flies. This type of fly, the Mallard, Teal, Woodcock and Grouse series, were all traditionally used, and still are, on the Scottish lochs. Apart from these flies, we can add some specific patterns devised to be wet sedge imitations. They were usually termed as flies for the gloaming, or Evening flies. Many of the Scottish rivers had styles of flies named after them, such as the Tummel, the Dee, the Tweed and, of course, the Clyde style of fly, which is perhaps the best known.

In 1885 David Webster published his book *The Angler and the Loop Rod*, a book containing a wealth of information on the type of flies for the Clyde and associated streams. The Grannom is to be found in his list, along with a fly called the Autumn Musk Fly, a fly which is a fair representation of the Cinnamon Sedge. It is an interesting fact that this sedge does not get its name from a cinnamon colour, but from the fact that it is supposed to smell faintly of cinnamon. The late David Jacques felt it smelt more like geranium. Whenever I have cupped such a sedge in my hand and given it a hearty sniff, all I can smell is my pipe tobacco. When I finally give up my little weakness, I may well be able to offer an opinion one way or the other. One must assume that this Scottish version of the sedge obtains its name from the aroma it emits, which, to someone, was perhaps reminiscent of musk.

The Autumn Musk

THE AUTUMN MUSK

DRESSING

Hook	Mustad 94841 sizes 10–12
Thread	Yellow
Body	Yellow silk
Hackle	Ginger hen
Wing	Light cock pheasant wing

Another of Webster's patterns was used as a gloaming fly and fits quite nicely into the sedge mould.

Evening Teal

EVENING TEAL

DRESSING

Hook	Mustad 94841 sizes 10–12
Thread	Yellow
Body	Yellow silk

Hackle   Light ginger hen
Wing   Mottled teal

Another Musk Fly is also given with a slightly different dressing. One can assume that this also is one of the Limnephilids.

THE MUSK BROWN

DRESSING

Hook   Mustad 94841 sizes 8–10
Thread   Yellow
Body   The downy fur of a hare's breast
Hackle   Light ginger hen
Wing   Light brown hen wing quill

The final Scottish fly I shall give is also a traditional evening fly. It is called the Pheasant Wing.

THE PHEASANT WING

DRESSING

Hook   Mustad 94841 sizes 8–10
Thread   Black
Body   Mixed black and brown wool
Hackle   Black hen
Wing   Light cock pheasant wing

Sea-trout fishermen, who stand in the rivers at night like nocturnal herons, sharing the time with inquisitive owls, flitting bats and fluttering sedges, and listening for the lusty splash of that prince among fish, were quick to appreciate the value of sedge patterns. Many of the old Welsh flies were used for this purpose, sometimes worked alone through an ink-black pool, or accompanied by a juicy maggot or a bronze wriggling gilt-tailed worm.

In the early 1920s, in Denmark, two gentlemen by the names of Krogsgaard and Findal devised a series of flies based on the insects found on their local rivers. The flies became known as the Krogsgaard series and many of them are sedges. The patterns number 1–9 and numbers 3, 4, 7, and 8 all have antennae, so, based on this, I may be forgiven for assuming them to be sedges of some sort. I believe that No. 4 is a Black Silverhorn. As for the others, your guess is as good as mine. They were used for all species of trout and grayling.

Step by step: Knogsgaard

KROGSGAARD NO. 3

DRESSING

Hook	Mustad 3904a sizes 4–12
Thread	Brown pre-waxed
Body	Chocolate-brown floss
Hackle	Natural dark red tied collar-style after the wing
Wing	Two strips of white hen or duck quill flanked by two strips of brown hen quill
Antennae	Bronze mallard

METHOD

Step 1 Take the thread down the hook and tie in a length of chocolate-brown floss silk. (I prefer to use wool as I get a nice plump body much quicker this way.) Return the tying thread up the shank.

Step 2 Form the body and trim off any excess silk or wool.

Step 3 Select two slips of white hen or duck quill and two slips of brown hen. Place the white slips inside the brown and tie in on top of the hook with the pinch and loop (soft loop) method.

Step 4 Take two strands of bronze mallard and tie them in so that they project over the eye of the hook.

Step 5 Wind on the hen hackle, or a soft cock hackle. Finish the fly in the usual way.

KROGSGAARD NO. 4

DRESSING

Hook	Mustad 3904a sizes 4–12
Thread	Black pre-waxed
Body	Woodcock quill
Hackle	Black hen (collar)
Wing	Jackdaw or moorhen
Antennae	Two strands of black horsehair.

KROGSGARD NO. 7

DRESSING

Hook	Mustad 3904a sizes 4–12
Thread	Brown pre-waxed
Body	Chocolate-brown floss (or wool)
Hackle	Ginger hen
Wing	Four blue dun hackle points
Antennae	Two strands of brown horsehair

KROGSGAARD NO. 8

DRESSING

Hook	Mustad 3904a sizes 4–12
Thread	Brown pre-waxed
Body	Brown raffia (or brown floss)
Hackle	Light red hen
Wing	Grey turkey dyed mauve
Antennae	Two strands of brown horsehair

The wide range of hook sizes is to cover all the fishing contingencies from sea-trout to grayling.

1

A useful book by Jesus Pariente Diez, called *La Pesca De La Trucha*, gives a number of traditional Spanish flies, some of which are considered to be sedge patterns. In the old days these flies were used as a team and fished, more often than not, by means of a bubble float of sorts. Nowadays, of course, most people use the conventional fly lines, although the bubble float method is still used in certain areas. Another style of fishing uses ultra-long rods with a fixed line at the top. The flies are worked in a semi-dapping method, across and downstream. A similar method of fishing was practised in northern Italy, using very similar spider-dressed flies. The following wet flies are traditional spider-dressed sedge patterns from the province of Leon.

2

3

MARCIAL

DRESSING

Hook	Mustad 3904a sizes 10–12
Thread	Green
Body	Grey silk
Rib	White silk
Hackle	*Pardo corzuno*
Head	Green

4

5

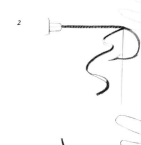

FALANGISTA

DRESSING

Hook	Mustad 3904 sizes 10–12
Thread	Black
Body	Black silk
Rib	Red silk
Hackle	Blackish-grey

6

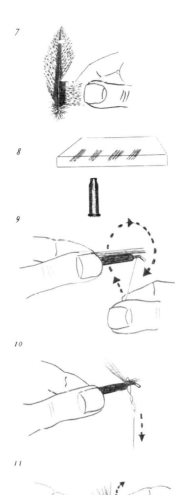

7

8

9

10

11

TYING IN THE SPANISH STYLE

The traditional Spanish flies were generally tied by using small hand vices adapted from a jeweller's vice. A number of bodies are tied up and the hackles applied afterwards. The last time I went to Spain I watched the dexterity of a Spanish fly dresser tying these patterns in the old traditional way, part with a hand vice and part by fingers alone. The resultant flies were all perfect replicas of each other. From my notes, made at the time, I have tried to repeat most of the procedures he used.

METHOD

Step 1   The first thing that is different in the tying of these flies is the fact that the hook is placed in the vice head first (note the adaptation in the jaws of the vice in order to accept the eye of the hook).

Step 2   The next stage I have adapted slightly, as I find it easier. Take the tying thread and wind it down the hook and then tie in a length of silk and a piece of fine tying thread or silk for the rib. Return the tying thread back towards the eye.

Step 3   Now form the tapered body by winding the silk up the hook.

Step 4   Tie off the body silk by means of a half hitch taken right over the body.

Step 5   Take the ribbing silk up the body and tie off in the same way.

Step 6   Quite often the whole silk body is varnished and then set aside to await the hackle procedure.

HACKLE PROCEDURE

Step 7   Select a hackle and tear off about five bunches of fibres.

Step 8   Separate all these fibres into equal bunches (these can be made equal by tamping them in an old 0.22 bullet case in much the same way you would use a hair stacker). For some patterns fibres from different coloured hackles can be used.

Step 9   Pick up one bunch and tie it in on top of the hook. Repeat with all the bunches.

Step 10   After the bunches have been tied in, with the thumb and finger of the right hand twist the fibres so that they spread around the hook (see 10a).

Step 11   Finish off the fly with a small neat head and a whip finish. Finally, varnish to secure.

Compared to the experts in this style of dressing, my attempts may appear to be somewhat crude, but like everything else in life practice makes perfect. I have always found it a worth-while exercise to try out fly patterns from other countries to see if they work on our home-grown trout. More often than not they do, for a good fly is usually effective everywhere. There are exceptions, of course. Sometimes an absolute killer can turn out to be something of a damp squib when fished on a water far from its birth, but you do not know this until you try it out. The famed Killer Bug of Frank Sawyer probably takes more grayling on British waters than any other fly, but try using it on the grayling of the rivers of Yugoslavia; the results are sadly disappointing.

Elsewhere in the book I give a number of patterns from the republic of Slovenia in Yugoslavia. Other places also have a history of fly fishing, such as Macedonia, Croatia and Bosnia. In 1897 the great English angler Skues took a fishing trip in Bosnia, lasting about sixteen days. He describes this at some length, along with some of the flies and methods used in that area of the Balkans in his book *The Chalk Stream Angler* (Seeley Service, 1932). Recently a Bosnian writer, Savo Martinovic, sent to me a number of Bosnian patterns, one of which can be described as a wet sedge pattern. It is called *Cǔk*, an onomatopoeic word for the cry of a small owl, feathers from which make up the wing. Most of the flies sent to me are virtually the same as in Skues's day, without eyes and on lengths of nylon leader (in Skues's time they used horsehair lines and gut casts, fishing four flies at a time, usually downstream).

THE CǓK

DRESSING

Hook	Tied direct to nylon, eyeless size 10
Thread	Brown
Body	Dark green silk
Rib	Brown silk
Hackle	None
Wing	Light brown mottled owl feather

The Cǔk

Marcial

CHAPTER TEN

Tying the Dry Sedge

In my opinion, fishing with a dry sedge pattern is one of the most exciting aspects of our pursuit of trout, whether it is for pink streaked rainbows on some large reservoir – those silver fish that leap amidst a rainbow of water droplets in an effort to rid themselves of the annoying hook – or maybe for some dark spotted brown trout, lying hard behind a rock in a crystal pool, ever alert for danger and as wild and wise as the river itself. To catch these fish on a sedge fly is a rewarding experience in itself, but part of the pleasure of catching the fish is the time spent at the fly-vice creating flies that will prove the downfall of all the fish of one's dreams. Over the years I have been given sedge patterns from all over the fly-fishing world, for nowadays the world of fly fishing is an international one and sedge patterns figure in the fly wallets of anglers from Alaska to Australia. In this chapter I will confine myself to the flies of the British Isles and leave the wealth of patterns from the USA and Europe to subsequent chapters.

A glance at the pre-war (1939–45) catalogues of some of the famed fly-dressing suppliers will give an indication as to the type of traditional dry sedge used on British rivers. I have looked at the catalogues of Hardy's, Farlow's, Ogden Smith's and others of this period and the thing that is most noticeable is their bias towards the flies for the lush southern chalk streams and the still evident influence of such fly fishermen as Halford. These traditionally dressed dry sedges have, in recent years, been criticised as inconsistent; sometimes they caught trout and sometimes they did not. There is a degree of validity in the criticism, in as much as the style of winging (in some instances they were even tied with upright wings) was not very realistic. Two slips of feather placed back to back does nothing for the appearance of the fly when viewed from underneath. Today the imitations of the sedge have a far better configuration, a more realistic silhouette and a far better success rate in tempting the trout. Nevertheless, it is worth recording these traditional flies, for they are part of our fly-tying heritage.

THE TRADITIONAL DRY SEDGE

THE SILVER SEDGE (*Odontocerum albicorne*)

DRESSING

Hook	Mustad 3913b up-eyed sizes 10–14
Thread	Black
Body	White floss silk
Rib	Silver wire
Hackle	Palmered ginger along the body, ginger at the head
Wing	Landrail substitute or grey duck

THE CINNAMON SEDGE (*Limnephilus lunatus*)

DRESSING

Hook	Mustad 3913b up-eyed sizes 10–12
Thread	Brown
Body	Cinnamon turkey feather fibre
Rib	Gold wire
Hackle	Palmered ginger cock along the body, ginger at the head
Wing	Landrail substitute

THE GRANNOM (*Brachycentrus subnubilus*)

DRESSING

Hook	Mustad 3913b size 14
Thread	Green
Body	Grey/brown hare's ear with a tip of green wool at the tail
Hackle	Rusty dun (tied after the wing)
Wing	Hen pheasant wing

Grannom

THE BROWN SEDGE (*A PATTERN REPRESENTING A NUMBER OF SEDGES*)

DRESSING

Hook	Mustad 3913b size 14
Thread	Orange

Body	Dubbed brown and fawn wool
Hackle	Natural red cock
Wing	Natural red hen wing quill

Kimbridge

THE KIMBRIDGE SEDGE (*NAMED AFTER A WELL-KNOWN STRETCH OF THE TEST*)

DRESSING

Hook	Mustad 3913b sizes 10–14
Thread	Black
Body	White wool
Rib	Fine silver wire
Hackle	Palmered light red cock hackle
Wing	Woodcock wing quill

THE ORANGE SEDGE (*A HALFORD PATTERN*)

DRESSING

Hook	Mustad 3913b sizes 10–14
Thread	Orange
Body	Orange floss silk
Rib	Fine gold wire
Hackle	Palmered ginger cock
Wing	Landrail substitute

There are many dressing variations given for the above-listed flies. Other sedge flies, which are considered classic traditional patterns, are given with more up-to-date modern dressings on pages 103–4.

THE CLIPPED HACKLE SEDGES OF J. T. H. LANE

The book *Lake & Loch Fishing* by Joscelyn Lane, published in the mid-1950s, is a book written with a light hand and a gentle sense of humour by a man who obviously loved his fishing. His observations on insect and fish behaviour were probably ahead of his time. The designs of his floating sedge patterns were certainly unique; the use of clipped cock hackle bodies as an aid to floatability is certainly worthwhile recording here.

LANE'S CINNAMON SEDGE (*Limnephilus lunatus*)

DRESSING

Hook	Mustad 94840 size 10
Thread	Golden olive pre-waxed
Tail	Pale ginger cock hackle fibres
Body	Clipped ginger cock hackle fibres
Thorax	Clipped ginger cock hackle fibres
Wing	Pale ginger cock hackle fibres
Hackle	Ginger cock hackle

LANE'S MOTTLED CINNAMON SEDGE (*Limnephilus marmoratus*)

DRESSING

Hook	Mustad 94840 size 10
Thread	Golden olive pre-waxed
Tail	Rusty-dun cock hackle fibres
Body	Clipped natural red cock hackle
Thorax	Clipped natural red cock hackle fibres
Wing	Rusty-dun cock hackle fibres
Hackle	Natural red cock hackle

The natural sedge (*L. marmoratus*) is quite a common species. It can be found locally in quite large numbers both in the UK and throughout most of Europe.

METHOD

Step 1 Take the tying thread down the hook and tie in a bunch of hackle fibres for the tail. Keeping the butts level, trim the hackle fibres straight.

Step 2 At the tail end tie in a large cock hackle. Return the thread up the shank to about half-way and follow with the palmered hackle. Tie off and remove any surplus hackle. The turns of the hackle must closely touch one another, but not overlap.

Step 3 Trim the hackle flush with the hook shank on the top, and trim the bottom and sides approximately to the length depicted in the sketch.

Step 4 Tie in a bunch of cock hackles for the wing. No light should show between the body and the wing and tail. Trim the wing fibres to the end of the tail.

Step 5 For the thorax tie in another cock hackle over the roots of the wing, and palmer towards the eye, leaving enough room for the final hackle. Trim the thorax hackle to a conical shape.

Step 6 Tie in the final hackle and leave it untrimmed. Finish the fly in the usual way, with a whip finish and a touch of varnish.

The smaller sedges of Joscelyn Lane were tied in the same way, but they did not have the tail fibres. The large sedges were fished dry and the smaller patterns were fished as both wet and dry flies. They were treated with floatant for dry and left untreated if they were to be used as wet patterns. The dressings are as follows:

LANE'S SMALL BROWN SEDGE (*A GENERAL BROWN SEDGE PATTERN*)

DRESSING

Hook	Mustad 94840 sizes 12–14
Thread	Golden olive pre-waxed
Body	Clipped ginger cock hackle
Wing	Brown partridge fibres
Hackle	Natural red cock hackle

LANE'S SMALL RED SEDGE (*Tinodes waeneri*)

DRESSING

Hook	Mustad 94840 sizes 12–14
Thread	Hot orange pre-waxed
Body	Clipped ginger cock hackle
Wing	Pale ginger cock hackle
Hackle	Natural red cock hackle

LANE'S LITTLE BLACK SEDGE (*Berae pullata*)

DRESSING

Hook	Mustad 94840 sizes 12–14
Thread	Black pre-waxed
Body	Clipped black cock hackle
Wing	Black cock hackle fibres
Hackle	Black cock hackle

The sedge *B. pullata* appears to be fairly common right throughout Europe, but according to McLachlan it would seem to be localised in the UK. Lane recommends its use for Welsh tarns. The sedge itself favours a shallow water habitat. The size of the wing is about 6 mm. As one would expect from the dressing, the natural colour is a very dark grey to black.

LANE'S SMALL SILVER SEDGE (*Lepidostoma hirtum*)

DRESSING

Hook	Mustad 94840 sizes 12–14
Thread	Straw colour pre-waxed
Body	Clipped honey cock hackle
Wing	Pale blue-dun cock hackle fibres
Hackle	Pale ginger cock

LANE'S MEDIUM SEDGE (*Goera pilosa*)

DRESSING

Hook	Mustad 94840 size 12
Thread	Straw colour pre-waxed
Body	Clipped dark honey-dun cock hackle
Wing	Medium honey-dun cock hackle fibres
Hackle	Ginger cock hackle

THE RICHARD WALKER SEDGE PATTERNS

We have already encountered some of Richard Walker's innovative fly patterns. The following sedges, I believe, owe something to the Joscelyn Lane flies given above, in as much as both adopt light hackle fibre wings for realism. Very few angling writers have had the impact on freshwater fishing of the late Richard Walker. His writings have ensured him a place in angling history and the fly patterns he created are a legacy for all those who will come after him. While he was alive he held his place at the top of the angling ladder, while the rest of us remained somewhat in his shadow.

I will give just five of his adult sedge patterns.

WALKER'S CINNAMON SEDGE

DRESSING

Hook	Mustad 94842 (or on long shank) sizes 10–12
Thread	Hot orange pre-waxed
Butt	Yellow fluorescent floss
Body	Buff ostrich herl
Rib	None (I tend to use a fine gold wire as ostrich herl tends to be delicate)
Wing	Cree cock hackle fibres
Hackle	Ginger or light red cock hackle

WALKER'S LARGE BROWN SEDGE

DRESSING

Hook	Mustad long shank 79580 size 10
Thread	Orange pre-waxed
Butt	Fluorescent yellow floss
Body	Dark brown ostrich herl
Wing	Light brown hackle fibres
Hackle	Light brown hackle fibres

WALKER'S GROUSE WING

DRESSING

Hook	Mustad long shank 79580 sizes 12–14
Thread	Black pre-waxed
Butt	White fluorescent silk
Body	Chocolate ostrich or dyed swan herl
Wing	Grouse wing or tail fibres
Hackle	Dark furnace

WALKER'S RED SEDGE

Walker's Red Sedge

DRESSING

Hook	Mustad long shank 79580 size 10
Thread	Orange pre-waxed
Body	Chestnut-brown ostrich
Wing	Natural red cock hackle fibres
Butt	Arc chrome fluorescent wool
Hackle	Natural red cock hackle

Sometimes this pattern is tied with a green body, to imitate those natural sedges that have this distinct green coloration.

WALKER'S SMALL BUFF SEDGE

DRESSING

Hook	Mustad long shank 79580 size 12
Thread	Primrose pre-waxed
Body	Buff ostrich herl or swan herl
Wing	Buff cock hackle fibres
Hackle	Two buff cock hackles

The Walker sedges are extremely easy to tie; the thing to note is that the wing fibres are clipped level with the bend of the hook.

THE TERRY THOMAS DEER WING SEDGES

Terry Thomas, the well-known angling writer and broadcaster, created a set of deer-hair patterns to represent a number of different sedge species. His deer-hair flies were created long before many other such flies in the UK. He was one of the first to appreciate the buoyant nature of deer hair used in the construction of the wings of his flies.

THE DARK SEDGE (THOMAS)

DRESSING

Hook	Mustad 3904a sizes 12–14
Thread	Black pre-waxed
Body	Black wool or chenille with a palmered black hackle
Wing	Black deer hair
Hackle	Black cock hackle

THE LIGHT SEDGE (THOMAS)

DRESSING

Hook	Mustad 3904a sizes 12–14
Thread	Brown pre-waxed
Body	Light cock pheasant tail fibres, palmered with a ginger cock hackle
Wing	Brown deer hair
Hackle	Ginger cock hackle

STANDARD SEDGE (THOMAS)

Terry Thomas Sedge

DRESSING

Hook	Mustad 3904a sizes 12–14
Thread	Brown pre-waxed
Body	Dark cock pheasant tail fibres with a palmered ginger cock hackle
Wing	Natural grey deer hair
Hackle	Ginger cock

SKITTER SEDGES

I based these flies on an American pattern shown to me by Darrel Martin in the summer of 1987. I adapted the original to suit Britain's natural sedges and for use on large reservoirs. The resultant flies proved highly successful wherever I used them. I published the original fly in *Trout Fisherman* magazine at the end of 1987. I can assure the reader that these flies are highly effective and are worth giving a try. The secret of these flies lies in the unique style of winging.

THE SKITTER GREY SEDGE (*Odontocerum albicorne*)

DRESSING

Hook	Mustad 3904a sizes 8–10
Thread	Black or grey pre-waxed
Body	Grey Antron or alternative dubbing
Wing	Natural deer hair
Hackle	Grey or blue-dun
Antennae	Mose body hair

THE SKITTER BLACK SILVERHORN (*SUITABLE FOR ANY OF THE BLACK SEDGES*)

DRESSING

Hook	Mustad 3904a sizes 10–12
Thread	Black pre-waxed
Body	Black Antron or alternative
Wing	Black deer hair
Hackle	Black cock hackle
Antennae	Two strands of teal flank

THE SKITTER GROUSE WING (*Mystacides longicornis*)

DRESSING

Hook	Mustad 3904a sizes 10–12
Thread	Brown pre-waxed
Body	Brown Antron or alternative
Wing	Light brown deer hair, marked with bands of black by means of a waterproof pen
Hackle	Natural brown cock
Antennae	Two strands of brown mallard flank

THE SKITTER BROWN SILVERHORN (*Athripsodes cinereus*)

DRESSING

Same as the Grouse Wing but without the banding on the wing.

THE SKITTER CINNAMON SEDGE (*Limnephilus lunatus*)

Step by step: Skitter Sedge

DRESSING

Hook	Mustad 3906b size 8–10
Thread	Light brown pre-waxed
Body	Light brown or cinnamon Antron, alternatively green/brown Antron mixture
Wing	Cinnamon or light-brown-dyed deer hair
Hackle	Ginger cock hackle
Antennae	Moose body hair

1

THE SKITTER BROWN SEDGE (*SUITABLE FOR ANY OF THE BROWN SEDGES*)

DRESSING

Hook	Mustad 3906b sizes 8–10
Thread	Brown pre-waxed
Body	Brown Antron
Wing	Brown-dyed deer hair
Hackle	Brown cock hackle
Antennae	Moose body hair

2

THE SKITTER GRANNOM (*Brachycentrus subnubilus*)

DRESSING

Hook	Mustad 3904a sizes 12–14
Thread	Brown pre-waxed
Body	First a turn of bright green Antron then brown Antron
Wing	Mixed brown and natural deer hair
Hackle	Cree cock hackle
Antennae	Two cock pheasant tail fibres, not too long

3

METHOD OF TYING THE SKITTER SEDGES

Step 1 Take the tying thread down the hook and dub a little of the appropriate coloured dubbing onto the thread.

Step 2 Form a small dubbing button around the shank and tie in a small tuft of the deer-hair wing.

Step 3 Dub some more fur onto the thread and wrap it around the shank over the roots of the first portion of the wing.

Step 4 Now tie in another tuft of deer. Repeat the process until the hook is filled, taking care to leave enough room for the hackle.

Step 5 Tie in the antennae so that they project over the eye, and also tie in the cock hackle.

4

5

6

Step 6 Wind on the hackle and complete the fly in the usual manner.

All the main anglers' sedges can be imitated by this multi-wing style. Viewed from beneath they afford a very good sedge-like silhouette, with the advantage of having a degree of light penetration through the wing itself.

Step by step: G & H Sedge

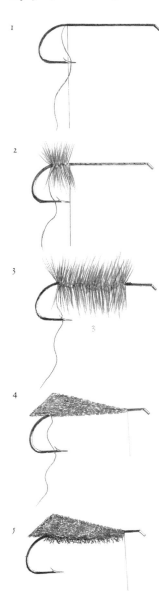

THE G&H SEDGE

The G&H Sedge was originated by John Goddard in collaboration with Cliff Henry at the time when both fished the Bough Beech Reservoir in Kent, a water that lies between Edenbridge and Sevenoaks. The fly is known in the United States as the Goddard Caddis. The fly itself is an extremely good floater, due, of course, to its solid clipped deer-hair wing. If a criticism must be made regarding this pattern, then it lies in the solid nature of the wing. It is very dense, allowing no light to come through. This criticism is a minor one, for most of the time trout are tempted to take the fly anyway; only the most selective of fish ignore the G&H Sedge.

DRESSING

Hook	Mustad 38941 long shank sizes 8–12 (or normal shank hooks)
Silk	Black or brown pre-waxed
Body	Green or brown seal's fur
Wing	Clipped deer hair
Hackle	Two natural red cock hackles, or light ginger for other colour variations
Antennae	Two hackle stalks left after tying in the hackles

METHOD

Step 1 Take the tying thread down the hook and there tie in a length of waxed thread.

Step 2 Cut off a small bunch of deer hair and spin it around the hook.

Step 3 Repeat the hair spinning for two-thirds of the hook. Tie off with a couple of half hitches and remove the hook from the vice.

Step 4 Trim the deer hair into the sedge wing shape. When complete, return the hook to the vice. Once more apply the tying thread to the hook.

Step 5 Dub some seal's fur onto the loose strand of thread tied in at Step 1 and take the fur-laden thread under the hook to form the abdomen of the fly.

Step 6 Tie in two cock hackles so that the stalks project over the eye.

Step 7 Wind on the hackles. Form a small neat head, separating the hackle stalk antennae. Finally trim off the top portion of the hackle.

As an alternative to the dubbed seal's-fur body, one can tie in a strand of wool of the appropriate colour in Step 1.

A light-coloured sedge can be tied by using grizzle hackles instead of the red or ginger.

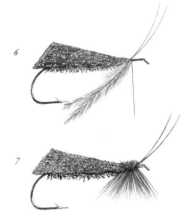

6

7

The large limestone lakes of Ireland have produced many fly patterns representing the family of sedges. It is on these lakes that the importance of the sedges as trout food was recognised far earlier than in many other parts of the British Isles. Perhaps the best known of these Irish patterns is the Murragh or Great Red Sedge. Many dressings are available for this fly. The one given below is typical.

THE MURRAGH (*Phryganae grandis* OR *P. striata*)

Murragh

DRESSING

Hook	Mustad 94841 size 8, or long shank 79580 sizes 10–12
Thread	Brown or black pre-waxed
Body	Chestnut-brown seal's fur or substitute
Rib	Fine oval gold
Wing	Dark speckled turkey, tied as a folded wing from one piece of feather strip. It is folded roof-like over the body and generally cut straight. The wing projects a little way beyond the bend of the hook
Hackle	Two natural red game-cock hackles
Antennae	Two strands of cock pheasant tail fibres about 1 in long.

The Caperer (*Halesus radiatus* or *H. digitatus*) is a big sedge by any standard. It is an autumnal sedge and a favourite of many stillwater anglers. It can be imitated by large versions of the Skitter Sedges given earlier, or by this pattern of mine which I have used for many years, generally with some degree of success.

THE CAPERER

Caperer

DRESSING

Hook	Mustad 79580 long shank sizes 8–10
Thread	Brown or orange pre-waxed
Body	Mixed orange seal's fur and hare's ear

Rib	Orange silk
Hackle	Palmered cree up the body, two cree at the head
Wing	Cree cock hackle fibres tied in the Walker sedge style of winging

THE MICRO-SEDGES

These small sedges, which can be of great importance on certain occasions when the trout start feeding selectively upon them, can be imitated by many of the patterns given but should be tied up in much smaller sizes, down to sizes 16 and 18. I have found the following patterns to be quite effective.

THE MICRO BLACK

Micro Black

DRESSING

Hook	Mustad 94841 sizes 16–18
Thread	Black pre-waxed
Hackle	Palmered black cock (there is no body as such)
Wing	A strip of any black feather folded in half and tied roof-style over the hackle

THE MICRO BROWN

DRESSING

Hook	Mustad 94841 sizes 16–18
Thread	Brown pre-waxed
Hackle	Palmered natural red cock hackle
Wing	A strip of brown feather folded as for the Micro Black

THE MICRO GREY

DRESSING

Hook	Mustad 94841 sizes 16–18
Thread	Black or grey pre-waxed
Hackle	Palmered grey cock hackle
Wing	A strip of grey duck folded as for the Micro Black

I have found these tiny sedge flies to be very effective during the day on both rivers and still water. It may well be that on occasions the trout take them because they are small and look like food. They may not take them just as sedges, but as a midge or even some small terrestrial beetle blown by accident onto the surface of the water. Whatever the case, these small flies should not be ignored by the angler, for they are certainly not ignored by the trout. The actual tying of the flies poses no great problem if you are used to tying on small hooks; the dressings themselves are pretty basic.

THE FLAT WING STYLE OF SEDGE

This type of winging lends itself very well to the sedge dry fly and also to imitations of the Plecoptera, the stoneflies. Any of the standard angler's sedges can be tied in this style. Appropriate game bird and hen hackles are used. These are prepared by varnishing with either clear cellulose or a vinyl adhesive. The following fly is such an example. I first published this fly in my book *Stillwater Flies Vol. 1*.

THE LARGE RED SEDGE (*Phryganae grandis* OR *P. striata*)

DRESSING

Hook	Mustad 79580 long shank 10
Thread	Brown pre-waxed
Body	Grey/brown polypropylene dubbing mix
Rib	Oval gold tinsel
Hackle	Palmered natural red cock, and two red cock at the head. The stalks are left untrimmed to act as antennae
Wing	Lacquered red hen body hackle, trimmed to shape

METHOD

Step 1 Take the thread down the shank and tie in a length of tinsel for the ribbing. Dub the fur onto the tying thread.

Step 2 Form the body by taking the fur-laden thread down the shank. Tie in a cock hackle and wind it down the body, securing with the ribbing tinsel. Take this tinsel up the body and tie off. Cut away any surplus tinsel and the hackle point at the tail end.

Step 3 Prepare the wing by coating the hen body feather with adhesive and stroking the fibres together. Trim the end of the feather by cutting a V-shape. Tie in on top of the hook.

Step 4 Wind on two hackles, leaving the stalks as antennae. Finish the fly with a whip finish and seal with a dab of varnish.

By using different hackles, such as grouse, partridge and pheasant body feathers, and varying the hackle shades, a whole range of sedges can be tied. This flat-wing style of fly looks very realistic when viewed from below as a trout would see it. Until I devised the Skitter range, I tended to use this type of fly a great deal on rivers.

Step by step: Large Red Sedge

1

2

3

4

The Welshman's Button (*Sericostoma personatum*) can be tied in the same way. The dressing is as follows.

THE WELSHMAN'S BUTTON

DRESSING

Hook	Mustad 94841 sizes 10–12
Body	Dark-chocolate-coloured turkey herl
Rib	Fine oval gold tinsel
Hackle	Palmered dark red game with collar of the same tied after the wing
Wing	Lacquered cock pheasant body feather

Wake Sedge

THE WAKE FLY STYLE OF SEDGE

As the light fades, some of the large sedges hatch from still water. Rather than fly off straightaway, they tend to trundle across the surface heading for the nearest bankside. Their progress is often marked by a distinct wake, and more often than not this miniature wake is followed by a much larger one as a cruising trout takes up the chase. The keynote of this style of dry sedge is activity. The fly is constructed so as to give the maximum disturbance at the water surface when it is retrieved. It is generally heavily hackled and with wings made from two cock hackles tied back to back so that they splay out. The following examples are broad-spectrum patterns imitating no specific natural, but they can be used to represent many of the larger nocturnal sedges.

THE BROWN WAKE FLY

DRESSING

Hook	Mustad 79850 sizes 8–12
Thread	Brown pre-waxed
Body	Heavily palmered natural red cock
Wings	Two natural red cock hackles, tied with the shiny side in so that they splay out
Antennae	The wing hackle stalks left untrimmed

THE FURNACE WAKE FLY

As above but with dark furnace hackles.

THE BLACK WAKE FLY

As above but with black hackles.

THE BADGER WAKE FLY

As above but with badger hackles.

THE GRIZZLE WAKE FLY

As above but with grizzle hackles.

One could go on *ad infinitum* with patterns imitating the sedges of the British Isles – there are so many – and I apologise to any reader whose favourite sedge pattern has been left out. I do feel, however, that I have given enough to satisfy the needs of most fly fishermen or fly tyers.

CHAPTER ELEVEN

EUROPEAN PATTERNS

The role of the sedge as a fishing fly is appreciated throughout the fly-fishing countries of Europe. France, Switzerland, Austria, Spain, Italy, Germany, Scandinavia and Yugoslavia all have their own sedge patterns. Many such flies have crossed international borders; in some instances they remain unchanged, in others they have been adapted to suit local conditions or local fly-tying materials. Many of the natural sedges found in such countries are the same species found in the British Isles, in some cases even keeping their British common name.

Many European countries have utilised duck preen-gland feathers in their fly patterns. These are often known by their French name, *culs de canard*. Fly dressers from France, Switzerland, Italy, Bavaria and Slovenia all resort to this feather as a method of adding floatability to some of their sedge flies. It is generally accepted that the use of such feathers originated in the Jura region of Switzerland. From there they crossed into France and to the rest of Europe. For a number of seasons now I, too, have used these grey wispy feathers as an integral part of many of my fishing flies.

It is strange how their use has been unknown, unaccepted or resisted by British fly dressers, as normally the British angler is quick to accept innovation. I think the reason lies in our actual fishing practice. In the rest of Europe far more anglers fish rivers and therefore use the dry fly as a matter of course. In Britain the greatest increase in fly fishing is to be found on the large manmade waters where the use of the dry fly is limited to a few specific times, i.e., the time of the sedge, of course, and the cranefly time, which are the two most important times. Try to change some of our chalk-stream anglers' flies and attitudes and you will come up against considerable resistance. In some areas tradition dies hard, and for most of the time this is no bad thing, but occasionally it is nice to have a little breeze to blow away the cobwebs; to part the Victorian curtains and let in the light and the twentieth century. Just as I have used foreign flies in the UK on all sorts of water, I have taken some British flies to European rivers and streams. Most of the time the fish take them well, for a trout is a trout is a trout and knows no borders, but just occasionally a local pattern seems to be more effective, although don't ask me why. It is one of the pleasurable mysteries of fishing.

AUSTRIAN SEDGES

THEN N. E. SEDGE

This pattern was devised by the late Norbert Eipeltauer of Vienna. A year or two ago he sent me a number of his patterns for a book I was working on. Among his flies were a couple of sedge patterns. This one is used for any of the medium to small brown sedges.

N. E. Sedge

DRESSING

Hook	Mustad 94841 sizes 10–14
Thread	Black pre-waxed
Body	Brown polypropylene dubbing (there is also a green version)
Hackle	Palmered brown cock hackle
Wing	Hen pheasant wing tied as a roof and clipped to shape

THE WHITE SEDGE

This is another of Eipeltauer's sedge flies. He told me that it was used sometimes as a moth imitation and was very effective as the light faded. Not only can it be seen by the trout, it is also seen by the angler. The American sedge pattern, the White Miller, is a similar fly. Eipeltauer also recommended this fly for grayling.

DRESSING

Hook	Mustad 94841 sizes 12–16
Thread	Black pre-waxed
Body	White wool or polypropylene dubbing
Hackle	Palmered white cock
Wing	White duck quill tied as a roof and clipped to shape

ROMAN MOSER SEDGE

Roman Moser is one of Europe's most talented fly dressers, and not afraid to use innovative materials in the make-up of his flies. This particular pattern makes use of the buoyant properties of deer hair.

Moser Sedge

DRESSING

Hook	Mustad 9672 or Partridge HIA sizes 8–12
Thread	Brown pre-waxed
Body	Deer hair bound down the shank
Hackle	Collar of deer hair
Wing	Traun River Products sedge wing
Head	Deer hair

MOSER'S FLUTTERING CADDIS

Worldwide there are a number of sedge imitations known as the Fluttering Caddis. This one by Roman Moser is as good as any using, as it does, deer hair for the wing.

DRESSING

Hook	Partridge Moser Sedge Hook sizes 12–16
Thread	Brown pre-waxed
Body	Traun body gill (see note)
Back	Thin foam plastic, grey in colour
Wings	Brown deer hair

BODY GILL

This material is supplied by Traun River Products and is basically a foam plastic which appears to be flocked on either one or both sides. A similar product can be found at a hardware shop in the guise of the material found on inexpensive paint rollers. (There are two main types of roller, the lambswool and the cheaper foam plastic alternative. I am referring to the latter.)

Moser seems to be an angling fly dresser with a sedge for all occasions. The next pattern imitates a surface-egg-laying female as she busies herself in dipping her abdomen through the surface film.

EGG-LAYING SEDGE

DRESSING

Hook	Mustad 94841 sizes 10–12
Thread	Brown pre-waxed
Body	Body gill material
Thorax	Thin plastic foam, flocked up with a needle to make it a little rough
Wing	Brown deer hair tied over the eye of the hook

Moser ties a range of conventional-looking sedges using Raffene as the winging medium. This artificial raffia is first varnished in order to keep it looking like a wing (untreated, the material tends to become soft and misshapen when wet). There are about half a dozen different colour variations in this Moser selection. I give three here.

Moser's Sedge

MOSER ADULT SEDGE (*BLACK*)

DRESSING

Hook	Mustad 94841 sizes 10–12
Thread	Black pre-waxed
Body	Black poly propylene dubbing and chopped up black deer hair, dubbed onto the tying thread
Thorax	As body, picked out to simulate legs
Wing	Black Raffene, varnished and clipped to shape

MOSER ADULT SEDGE (*BROWN*)

As the Black but substitute brown materials throughout.

MOSER ADULT SEDGE (*CINNAMON*)

As the Black, but with cinnamon materials.
   Others in the series are various shades of brown or grey.

Bavarian Sedges

I am indebted to Rudi Rubel for the following sedges which are used in Bavaria. These patterns by Rudi Rubel will catch fish anywhere. In one or two of his flies he uses the preen-gland feathers for extra flotation in the dressing. I feel sure that this is an influence from some of the sedges from Slovenia. Similar flies are to be found in Italy and also in Austria.

DARK SEDGE (*RUBEL*)

DRESSING

Hook	Mustad 94841 sizes 10–12
Thread	Black pre-waxed
Body	Dark grey dubbing or polypropylene
Wing	Black turkey or a similar feather backed by nylon (see Voljc sedges under Slovenian flies on page 00)
Hackle	Grey preen-gland feather (*culs de canard*)

Light Sedge (Rubel)

LIGHT SEDGE (*RUBEL*)

DRESSING

Hook	Mustad 94841 sizes 10–12
Thread	Brown pre-waxed
Body	Light buff polypropylene dubbing
Wing	Artificial wing material (various fly-dressing material suppliers offer such winging materials)
Hackle	Buff-coloured preen-gland feather
Antennae	Two grey duck wing feather fibres

DEER HAIR SEDGE (*RUBEL*)

Deer-Hair Sedge (Rubel)

DRESSING

Hook	Mustad 94841 sizes 10–12
Thread	Black pre-waxed
Body	Peacock herl
Wing	Natural deer hair
Hackle	Palmered grey preen gland
Head	Yellow poly-foam

PHEASANT SEDGE (*RUBEL*)

DRESSING

Hook	Mustad 94841 sizes 10–12
Thread	Black pre-waxed
Body	Fawn-coloured dubbing
Wing	Cock pheasant 'church window' lacquered for durability
Hackle	Grey preen gland feather

PREEN SEDGE (*RUBEL*)

DRESSING

Hook	Mustad 94841 sizes 10–12
Thread	Black pre waxed
Body	Grey dubbing (preen-gland feather fibre makes a good floating dubbing medium)
Wing	Preen-gland feathers
Hackle	Blue-dun cock hackle

SMALL GREY SEDGE (*RUBEL*)

DRESSING

Hook	Mustad 94841 sizes 12–14
Thread	Black pre-waxed
Body	Grey dubbing
Wing	Grey duck wing feather, nylon backed
Hackle	Grey preen-gland feather

SMALL BROWN SEDGE (*RUBEL*)

DRESSING

Hook	Mustad 94841 sizes 12–14
Thread	Brown pre-waxed
Body	Light brown dubbing
Wing	Mottled turkey, nylon backed (or similar feather)
Hackle	Brown cock hackle

Step by step: Palu's Yellow Sedge

ITALIAN SEDGES

I was given these sedges by Francesco Palu of Udine in north-east Italy. Palu's sedges fall into two types. One is a flat-wing type made from turkey wing slips backed to nylon, and the other type uses two lacquered slips of various feather fibres, tied in a distinct V-formation. He also ties a large sedge made up in the main from the hair of a wild boar. One evening I watched him use his sedges to catch what many considered to be uncatchable grayling on the trophy stretch of the River Unec in Slovenia. He stood on the bridge spanning the river and cast his sedge to a shoal of specimen grayling that were finning in the current. He allowed the sedge to float unmolested for a while. The fly was ignored by the fish. He then waved his rod in such a manner as to cause the fly to jump off the water surface and then fall back down, swirl one way, skip off, then swirl another way. Every grayling in the shoal raced the others to take this activated sedge. If it did nothing else, it proved that a fly that looks alive will be a successful pattern providing it is presented in a way that gives it apparent life. The following three of Palu's flies are just some of many he ties to represent a whole range of natural sedges.

PALU'S MOTTLED SEDGE

DRESSING

Hook	Mustad 94841 sizes 10–12
Thread	Black pre-waxed
Hackle	Heavily palmered preen gland and natural red cock hackles. These also form the body
Wing	Mottled turkey or similar, backed with nylon
Antennae	A few fibres of bronze mallard

PALU'S RED SEDGE

DRESSING

Hook	Mustad 94841 sizes 10–12
Thread	Brown pre-waxed
Tail	Short tuft of ginger cock hackle fibres
Body	Cream-coloured dubbing
Hackle	Ginger palmered down the body and at the head
Wing	Two strips of cinnamon turkey or a similar feather tied in a V across the back
Antennae	A few fibres of grey mallard

PALU'S YELLOW SEDGE

DRESSING

Hook	Mustad 94841 sizes 10–12
Thread	Yellow pre-waxed
Tail	A short tuft of light ginger cock hackle fibres
Body	Green dubbing
Hackle	Palmered light ginger and at the head
Wing	Two strips of cinnamon turkey or similar feather dyed yellow. The result gives an olive-yellow shade. Like the above pattern they are tied in a V.
Antennae	A few fibres of dyed mallard flank (yellowy-olive)

METHOD

Step 1 Take the thread down the hook and tie in a few ginger fibres for the tail. At the same place tie in a cock hackle by the tip. Dub some fur material onto the tying thread.

Step 2 Take the fur-laden thread down the shank to form the body.

Step 3 Wind on the palmered hackle.

Step 4 Tie in two strips of lacquered turkey feather, on top of the hook, in a V.

Step 5 Finish off by tying in a bunch of mallard feathers as the antennae, and then winding on the final hackle. Whip finish, varnish and the fly is complete.

Spotted guinea fowl feathers are used in a number of countries as the winging feather for sedges. Sometimes the wing quill is used, as in the next Italian pattern. At other times guinea fowl hackles are used, both plain and, in some cases, dyed. The feathers imitate sedges that are heavily spotted and marked in the natural state.

THE GUINEA FOWL SEDGE

Guinea Fowl Sedge

DRESSING

Hook	Mustad 94841 sizes 8–12
Thread	Black pre-waxed
Hackle	Heavily palmered grizzle with two grizzle at the head
Wing	Guinea fowl wing slip, lacquered for durability. The end of the wing is trimmed to shape and roofed over the body so that it projects beyond the bend of the hook

THE GREY SEDGE (*ITALIAN*)

DRESSING

Hook	Mustad 94841 sizes 8–12
Thread	Grey or black pre-waxed
Hackle	Palmered grey hackle, and grey at the head
Wing	Grey duck wing treated as in the last pattern

THE BLACK SEDGE (*ITALIAN*)

As for the grey sedge but substitute black materials.

FRENCH SEDGES

As in all the fly-fishing countries, patterns to represent the sedge are legion in France. They also show the same variety in design and in the materials used. There are feather-winged flies from the firm of Guy Plas in mid-France, solid winged flies in Normandy and in eastern France, close to the Swiss border, we see once more the ubiquitous *culs de canard* feathers being used by people like Devaux in the construction of some of his sedges. I am indebted to Raymond Rocher of Tain L'Hermitage for his help with some of this information. He is well known for his many articles in French and

British fishing magazines, as well as for his translations of British books into his native French.

The natural sedge *Philopotamus montanus* occurs in many areas of France, especially at altitude. It has been copied by fly dressers in a number of different ways. The first pattern I picked up in a French tackle shop some years ago. It uses a Guinea fowl hackle for the wing, dyed a yellowy-brown. This imitates the dark wing of *P. montanus*, complete with the natural spotting.

THE DARK SPOTTED SEDGE (*P. MONTANUS*)

DRESSING

Hook	VMC 9283 long shank size 12 or Mustad 38941 long shank size 12
Thread	Brown pre-waxed
Body	Brown dubbing
Wing	Guinea fowl hackle dyed yellowy-brown, trimmed to shape and lacquered for durability
Hackle	Natural red game at the head only

Woodcock Sedge

THE WOODCOCK WINGED SEDGE (*ROCHER*)

In larger sizes this sedge also imitates *P. montanus*, a sedge found in the south east and central France, usually at altitude between 1,300 to 3,300 ft. It generally emerges during the day. In smaller sizes this pattern can imitate a wide number of small dark sedges. Raymond Rocher ties them down to size 14, normal shank.

DRESSING

Hook	VMC 9283 long shank size 12 or normal shank down to size 14
Thread	Brown
Body	Brown silk
Wing	Woodcock body feather, in larger sizes trim to shape and lacquer.
Hackle	Dark natural red cock hackle

Partridge Sedge

THE PARTRIDGE WINGED SEDGE (*DEVAUX*)

This sedge is used as an imitation of the Small Silver Sedge (*Lepidostoma hirtum*). When tied in the smaller sizes on larger hooks it is used to imitate the Large Silver or Grey Sedge (*Odontocerum albicorne*).

DRESSING

Hook	VMC 9288 sizes 14–16 or in larger sizes
Thread	Brown
Body	Same as tying thread
Wing	Two grey partridge feathers flanking the hook, trimmed to shape and varnished for durability
Hackle	Dark ginger cock at the head only

Another of the Devaux patterns, tied to represent the Large Silver or Grey Sedge (*O. albicorne*), is the following fly. I am told it is a successful pattern on the eastern rivers of France.

THE SILVER GREY SEDGE (*DEVAUX*)

DRESSING

Hook	Mustad 9672 or similar sizes 12–14
Thread	Yellow
Body	As tying thread
Wing	Greyish-brown cock pheasant wing slips, varnished and clipped to shape
Hackle	Ginger cock

Among the patterns sent to me by Raymond Rocher was one from the French fly dresser Bresson. It is described as a night-time sedge and it resembles the American fly Carey's Special. It looks like a fly that will fish well in the surface film; a versatile pattern that can be fished on or below the surface.

THE BRESSON SEDGE (*PEUTE*)

DRESSING

Hook	Mustad 94841 size 12
Thread	Brown
Tag	Fluorescent orange floss
Body	Cock pheasant tail
Hackle	Cock pheasant rump feather (or hen mallard body feather)

Bresson Sedge

THE LIGHT SEDGE (*ROCHER*)

DRESSING

Hook	Mustad 94841 or similar sizes 10–12
Thread	Yellow
Body	As tying thread
Wing	Light coloured pheasant feather, varnished and clipped

to shape, flanking the hook.

Hackle   Ginger cock hackle

THE DARK SEDGE (*ROCHER*)

DRESSING

Hook   Mustad 94841 or similar sizes 10–12
Thread   Yellow
Body   As tying thread
Wing   Dark pheasant or similar feather, such as woodcock or
            grouse, varnished and clipped to shape
Hackle   Natural dark red cock

Mention has already been made of the *cul* feather. The following small sedge from the house of Devaux is a pattern utilising this wispy feather which needs no artificial floatant. The use by the French of this versatile feather can be traced over the border into Switzerland where the preen-gland feather was used for many many years on such flies as the Moustique series of dry flies.

Cul Sedge (Devaux)

CUL SEDGE (*DEVAUX*)

DRESSING

Hook   VMC 9288 or similar sizes 14–16
Thread   Yellow
Body   As tying thread
Wing   Dark game bird quill (pheasant, partridge, etc.) var-
            nished and clipped to shape, flanking the hook
Hackles   Natural red cock and preen-gland feather mixed, the
            preen gland is clipped to size

The firm of Guy Plas is situated in the Limousin area of France. On page 66 I gave a pattern for a pupa using the hackles from the cockerels of Limousin. All of Guy Plas's flies use these hackles – salmon, sea-trout, wet and dry flies are all tied with these superior feathers. Among the many dry flies supplied by the house of Plas is a sedge series called Phryganes which comes in a number of different shades of colour. The characteristic of these Plas sedges is the abbreviated body dressing.

PHRYGANES (*PLAS*)

Phryganes

DRESSING

Hook	VMC 9288 or similar, sometimes tied on long shank hooks
Thread	Grey
Body	Grey quill (short dressing)
Wing	Speckled rusty-grey hackle fibres
Hackle	Blue-grey hackle

Another broad-spectrum pattern from Guy Plas is the Pataude.

PATAUDE (*PLAS*)

DRESSING

Hook	Mustad 9672 long shank size 12
Thread	Brown
Body	Chestnut-brown herl, abbreviated dressing
Wing	Rusty-grey hackle fibres
Hackle	Rusty-grey

THE PRESKA SEDGE

The great French angler and hotelier Charles Ritz mentions the Preska Sedge in his excellent book *A Fly Fisher's Life*. This fly was created by T. Preskawiec to imitate a range of brown sedges. This was probably the first French sedge to adopt this type of roof winging. The fly was created after the last war and is still considered to be one of the most popular sedge patterns in France.

DRESSING

Hook	Mustad 94840 sizes 10–12
Thread	Brown pre-waxed
Body	Brown feather fibre (condor subs)
Wing	Brown mallard breast feathers tied on both sides of the shank, dull side in
Hackle	Brown cock hackle

SCANDINAVIAN SEDGES

The Krogsgaard series of flies given in Chapter 9 as wet flies can also be tied up as dry flies and used accordingly, but there are also a number of other patterns used in Scandinavia that are dry flies pure and simple. The first fly was created by an obvious fan of A. A.

Milne for the pattern is called Lumme's Nalle Puh (Lumme's Winnie the Pooh). The reason for the name is that the wings on the original pattern were made from cinnamon bear's hair. Nowadays it is more usual to see the fly tied with similar-coloured polypropylene fibres.

Lumme's Nalle Puh

NALLE PUH

DRESSING

Hook	Mustad 94841 sizes 8–14
Thread	Hot orange pre-waxed
Body	Mixed dubbing, comprising hare's ear, brown seal's fur and hot orange seal's fur tied around the bend
Rib	Fine round gold tinsel
Wing	Cinnamon bear or polypropylene
Hackle	Medium brown cock hackle

A pattern to imitate the Large Red Sedge (*Phryganae grandis*) is used by many Scandinavians for caching not only trout, but their prodigal brothers, the sea-trout. This pattern is given a tail. Don't ask me why, it may well be just for balance.

Laerdal

LAERDAL FLY (*SOMETIMES CALLED OLSEN'S LAERDAL FLY*)

Dressing	Mustad 94841 sizes 6–12
Thread	Black pre-waxed
Tail	Cock pheasant tail fibres not too long
Body	Heavily palmered light natural red cock hackle
Antennae	Badger hair (some call this the wing, but if it does represent the sedge then it is more likely to the antennae)

My good friend Sigverdt Steffensen of Tranbjerg in Denmark sent me a number of sedges tied by Karsten Fredrikson. The first three are tied in much the same way as the G&H Sedge on page 105 but are much smaller and clipped in a more cone-like shape and the deer hair is packed very tightly.

KARSTEN'S BROWN DEER-HAIR SEDGE

DRESSING

Hook	Mustad 94840 sizes 10–14
Thread	Brown pre-waxed
Body	Clipped deer hair dyed brown (this is, in fact, a wing also)
Hackle	Natural red cock
Antennae	Horsehair

KARSTEN'S CREAM DEER-HAIR SEDGE

As above but with a natural deer-hair body and a cream-coloured hackle.

Karsten's Mottled Deer-Hair Sedge

KARSTEN'S MOTTLED DEER-HAIR SEDGE

As above but with a body of mixed dyed coloured deer hair spun in bands of individual colours, and a hackle of blue-dun cock.

KARSTEN'S BLACK DEER-HAIR SEDGE

An all-black version of the above.

Karsten Fredrikson also ties a number of more conventional sedges using squirrel hair dyed in various colours for the wing. Another sedge sent to me by Sigverdt 'Steff' Steffensen was a pattern used all over Scandinavia – the Poly Sedge. This can be tied in a wide variety of colours.

RED POLY SEDGE

Red Poly Sedge

DRESSING

Hook	Mustad 94840 sizes 10–14
Thread	Brown pre-waxed
Body	Buff-coloured polypropylene dubbing
Wing	Reddish-brown sheet polypropylene clipped to shape
Antennae	Horsehair

SLOVENIAN SEDGES (*YUGOSLAVIA*)

Slovenia has a heritage of fly fishing and fly dressing equal to that of any country in Europe. Because of the fly-only rule for most of their waters, it makes this small republic in Yugoslavia one of the largest fly-fishing areas, per capita, in the world. The earliest recorded writing on fishing described the fishermen of Macedonia, now part of northern Greece and southern Yugoslavia, as using artificial flies. It could well be that the art of fly fishing has never left this part of the Balkans. If that is the case then their fly-fishing history is far longer than any of the acknowledged fly-fishing countries, Great Britain included. Whatever the truth of the matter, fly dressers in this part of Yugoslavia are turning out some quite remarkable and effective patterns. Their knowledge of the insect life found on their crystal-clear waters is reflected in their artificial flies. I have watched them tie flies and have fished alongside them, and I know from first hand just how good they are at both skills. As in other parts of Europe, their flies are generally tied with river fishing in mind.

Britain is the odd man out when it comes to fishing today, for we have developed our modern methods and skills on stillwater to the extent that we are second to none when fishing our lakes and reservoirs. I would not say that was true if you put us on rivers alone. I know a great number of very skilled fly fishermen who have rarely fished a river and can be quite lost when casting a fly for the first time on moving water. I suppose it is a question of horses for courses.

THE SLOVENIAN SEDGES OF DR VOLJČ

Dr Bozidar Voljč is probably Slovenia's leading fly-tying entomologist. His unique sedges and stoneflies are renowned throughout Europe and his methods of constructing his sedge patterns have been copied by many other fly tiers, myself included. The secret of the Voljč sedges lies in the winging, for not only are they almost indestructible, they have what can best be described as built-in buoyancy tanks, making them excellent floaters. Most of the common species of anglers' sedges are imitated by Dr Voljč. I will give his patterns first, then describe in detail his method of tying.

THE SILVER SEDGE (*SREBAČ*)

DRESSING

Hook	Mustad 94841 (or similar) sizes 14–16
Thread	Black pre-waxed
Body	Palmered ginger cock
Wing	Grey partridge or grey duck breast backed with nylon
Hackle	Ginger

THE GREY SEDGE (*SIVAŠ*)

DRESSING

Hook	Mustad 94841 (or similar) sizes 12–14
Thread	Black pre-waxed
Body	Palmered grizzle cock
Wing	Grey partridge hackle backed with nylon
Hackle	Grizzle

CINNAMON SEDGE (*CIMETAŠ*)

DRESSING

Hook	Mustad 94841 (or similar) sizes 12–18
Thread	Black pre-waxed

Body	Palmered ginger cock
Wing	Hen mallard body feather backed with nylon
Hackle	Dark ginger cock

This last pattern is used to imitate a wide variety of reddish sedges.

THE BLACK SEDGE (ČRNAȘ)

DRESSING

Hook	Mustad 94841 (or similar) sizes 12–16
Thread	Black pre-waxed
Body	Palmered black cock hackle
Wing	Black hen body feather backed with nylon
Hackle	Black cock

THE GRANNOM (ZELENAȘ)

DRESSING

Hook	Mustad 94841 (or similar) size 14
Thread	Black pre-waxed
Body	Palmered medium red
Wing	Brown mottled partridge backed with nylon
Hackle	Medium red

THE GREY FLAG (TREPETAČ)

DRESSING

Hook	Mustad 94841 (or similar)
Thread	Black pre-waxed
Body	Palmered dark blue-dun
Wing	Dark grey hen body feather or similar, backed, etc.
Hackle	Dark blue-dun

THE GROUSE WING (TIPAČ)

DRESSING

Hook	Mustad 94841 (or similar) sizes 14–16
Thread	Black pre-waxed
Body	Palmered medium red cock hackle
Wing	Woodcock or grouse hackle backed with nylon
Hackle	Medium red cock hackle

Step by step: Voljč Sedge

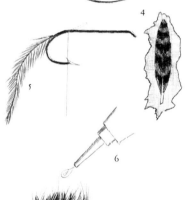

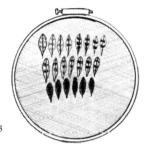

THE MOTTLED SEDGE (*MAVOGAČ*)

DRESSING

Hook	Mustad 94841 size 12
Thread	Black pre-waxed
Body	Palmered medium red cock
Wing	Brown mottled partridge backed with nylon
Hackle	Grizzle cock hackle

THE CAPERER (*PALETAŠ*)

DRESSING

Hook	Mustad 9672 long shank size 8
Thread	Black pre-waxed
Body	Palmered dark ginger cock
Wing	Cock pheasant flank feather backed with nylon
Hackle	Dark ginger cock hackle

Recent patterns by Dr Voljč have used a dubbed spun-fur front hackle, the hair coming from a dormouse tail, a fur which is extremely greasy and floats well. Another variant uses a preen-gland feather as a front hackle.

TYING THE VOLJČ SEDGES

First of all it is necessary to pre-form the wings. This is made easier by using an embroidery frame. Old nylon stocking material is stretched on the frame and trimmed around. The nylons available in Eastern Europe do not appear to be as elastic as the ones we have over here, so I tend to coat the stretched nylon with a thin clear dope. This stiffens it up somewhat and prevents contraction when released from the frame. The next stage is the preparation of the hackles. These, as you can see from the above dressings, are mainly game bird body feathers and hen back feathers. The feathers taken from crows, rooks, etc., can also be used – in fact anything that takes your fancy. Some of the sedges given earlier, from Italy and Bavaria, use slips taken from the wing quills instead of body feathers.

Dampen the body feathers slightly to shape them, coat the backs with clear PVC adhesive and then stick them neatly in rows onto the nylon. Fill up the whole frame with the prepared wings and allow them to dry before releasing the nylon from the frame. The bodies of the sedges are purely palmered hackles, the top tips of which are dotted with small drops of the same PVC adhesive just before applying the wing. The wings are cut around and trimmed underneath to the correct sedge wing shape then folded in half and tied in on top of the hook. The tips of the hackle adhere to the underside of the wing so that little pockets are formed beneath the wing. These little chambers trap the air, causing the fly to float reasonably well without the addition of a floatant. The final stage in the fly is the front hackle which is tied conventionally.

I picked up one or two more sedges on my last visit to Slovenia. Among them were the following. The first was given to me by Marjan Danush, a river warden on the wild River Radovna, a crystal-clear river of wild brown trout close to the tourist centres of Lake Bled and Bohinj and near the River Sava which pours out of Lake Bohinj. I still have the fly he gave me, in my fishing cap. He based it on an American pattern with a few adaptations of his own.

THE DANUSH SEDGE

DRESSING

Danush Sedge

Hook	Mustad 94841 sizes 10–14
Thread	Red pre-waxed
Tip	Red silk (or the tying thread exposed)
Body	Yellow floss silk
Hackle	Palmered grey or grizzle
Wing	Brown deer hair tied quite sparse

When one goes abroad to other fly-fishing countries, part of the enjoyment is swopping flies with the local anglers. I obtained the following flies late one night after a great deal of wine. They were given to me, through a haze of slivovitz, by Mr Gasparin whose pupa pattern I listed on page 61. The wings of these sedges are made of foxtail hair.

THE FOXTAIL SEDGE (NO. 1)

Gasparin Sedge

DRESSING

Hook	Mustad 94841 sizes 10–12
Thread	Black pre-waxed
Tail	Short bunch of cock hackle fibres
Body	Mixed red and brown seal's fur or substitute
Rib	Oval gold tinsel
Wing	Red foxtail hair
Hackle	Medium red cock hackle

THE FOXTAIL SEDGE (NO. 2)

DRESSING

Hook	Mustad 94841 sizes 10–12
Thread	Black pre-waxed
Tail	None
Body	Cream seal's fur or substitute
Rib	Black thread
Wing	Red foxtail hair
Hackle	Honey cock hackle

THE FOXTAIL SEDGE (NO. 3)

DRESSING

Hook	Mustad 94841 sizes 10–12
Thread	Black pre-waxed
Tail	None
Body	As No. 1
Rib	Oval gold tinsel
Wing	Red foxtail hair
Hackle	Honey cock hackle

THE FOXTAL SEDGE (NO. 4)

DRESSING

Hook	Mustad 94841 sizes 10–12
Thread	Black pre-waxed
Tail	None
Body	As No. 1
Rib	Oval gold tinsel
Wing	Foxtail hair, as dark as possible
Hackle	Dark grizzle cock

Fratnik's Sedge

FRATNIK SEDGES

Marjan Fratnik was born in the village of Most Na Soči (Bridge on the Soča) but now resides in Milan. His 'F' flies are famed throughout Europe and are constructed out of preen-gland feathers (cul de canard). His sedges also utilise this versatile feather.

FRATNIK'S GREY SEDGE

DRESSING

Hook	Mustad 90840 sizes 12–14 or a 1x long shank
Thread	Grey pre-waxed
Body	Thin grey synthetic dubbing
Hackle	Palmered grey along the body, grey also at the head (or grizzle)
Wing	Two preen-gland feathers tied slightly longer than the hook

FRATNIK'S BROWN SEDGE

As above, but substitute brown materials.

FRATNIK'S BLACK SEDGE

As above, but substitute black materials.

As you can see, these Fratnik sedges differ from those of Devaux in as much as in the French sedge the feather is used in the hackle, while the Fratnik sedges use the feather in the wing.

SWISS SEDGES

The following patterns were sent to me by Roland Heriegle of Interfly of Zurich. They are just two of a series of sedges under the name Universal, or to be more precise Universelles. The winging of these sedges is slightly different to most of the other sedges given so far. Two slips of feather are used. They do not flank the body as in some of the French flies, neither are they placed back to back as in the traditional English method. They are, in fact, rested flat on top of the hook. The natural outward curve of the feather provides the sedge-like wing shape without resorting to trimming as with some of the other patterns already given. The Universelles series of sedges are used in many European countries with slight variations in the dressing. I believe they originated in Belgium.

UNIVERSELLE (NO. 1)

DRESSING

Hook	Mustad 38930 sizes 10–14
Thread	Black pre-waxed
Body	Light green strip of PVC
Wing	Hen pheasant wing quill slips set on top of the hook so

that the ends form a natural V extending beyond the bend of the hook

Hackle   Natural red game with a white cock hackle in front

UNIVERSELLE (NO. 2)

DRESSING

Hook	Mustad 38930 sizes 10–14
Thread	Black pre-waxed
Body	Yellow plastic foam sheeting (see note)
Rib	Clear nylon monofilament
Wing	Hen pheasant as in No. 1
Hackle	Dark natural red cock hackle

FLY DRESSING NOTE

The fine foam used in the above pattern is available from many fly-dressing houses. At one time I used to purchase various colours from Germany. Nowadays, among the other suppliers, Traun River Products have a good range. It is a useful product for dry flies and emergent nymphs. I also use it for a range of floating terrestrial flies and beetles.

SPANISH SEDGES

The sedge is a favourite fly of many Spanish fly fishermen. I gave a couple of dressings of traditional-style sedges on page 92. As in most countries both traditional and modern patterns are used. The following pattern is one very similar to the Guy Plas Sedge. I obtained the fly from my good friend Victor Salt Santiago of Madrid, a giant among fishermen in fact, he is so tall, I could get into his chest waders twice.

VICTOR'S SEDGE

Victor's Sedge

DRESSING

Hook	Mustad 94841 sizes 10–14
Thread	Brown pre-waxed
Body	Cock pheasant centre tail fibres
Wing	Hackle fibres from a spade hackle of the *coqs de Leon* colour *flor de escoba* or *sarrioso*. The mottling matches the markings of some sedges
Hackle	Dark red game

The following sedges were given to me by Luis Antunez Jr. of Madrid.

SARRIOSA (ANABOLIA NERVOSA)

Hook	Mustad 94840 sizes 10–14
Thread	Brown pre-waxed
Body	In two halves, rear green silk, the rest yellow silk
Wing	Natural deer hair
Hackle	Natural red cock

BLACK SEDGE (TRICHOPTERA NEGRO)

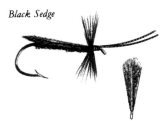

Black Sedge

Hook	Mustad 94840 sizes 12–14
Thread	Black pre-waxed
Body	Black polypropylene or similar
Hackle	Black cock
Wing	The base of a black hackle cut to shape
Antennae	Two fine black hackle stalks

HI-FLOAT SEDGE

Hook	Mustad 94840 sizes 10–14
Thread	Black or brown pre-waxed
Body	Brown clipped deer hair
Wing	Natural deer hair
Hackle	Dark blue dun

CHAPTER TWELVE
AMERICAN CADDIS PATTERNS

The influence of American fly design on British fishermen and British flies over the last twenty years has been profound. This is why I have included a chapter devoted to the American sedge patterns. In the early days of American fly fishing it was the British and European fly that was used. Now the reverse is true and many anglers in the UK are using American flies or at least patterns that have been influenced by an original American conception, such as the Muddler Minnow. This is a fly that is now found throughout Europe, as are some American sedge patterns.

Due to the immense size of the USA, its variation in climate and, of course, the number of different species to be found within its borders, it is not surprising that the number of patterns tied to imitate American caddis flies can run into many many hundreds, if not thousands. The flies given in this chapter can only be a representative selection embracing both traditional and modern imitations, in keeping with the other selections given in the chapters on British and European sedges.

The traditional American sedge is similar both in style and in the materials used to its British counterpart, and it must be true to say that these days its use is more or less confined to diehard traditionalists, for more modern ideas, by way of dressing and fly style, have superseded these older flies. Having said this, I still think it worth while recording a few of them, just for the record, and for comparison's sake. Historical classic flies are the foundation of today's patterns. I think it was Churchill who more or less said that a country which ignores its history will have no future. This statement can also apply to our sport

TRADITIONAL AMERICAN PATTERNS

This first pattern has been tied and fished as a wet and a dry fly. It is called the White Miller and is an artificial tied to represent the American caddis genus *Nectopsyche*, of which there are about twelve species. They are generally night-time emergers. There are many dressing variations of this fly; some with a pale green body and one with an orange tip to the abdomen. The following pattern is the simple all-white version.

AMERICAN WHITE MILLER (*Nectopsyche albida*, ETC.)   *White Miller*

DRESSING

Hook	Mustad 94840 sizes 10–12
Thread	White pre-waxed
Body	White floss silk
Rib	Fine silver tinsel
Wing	White duck (for some reason or another these wings were set upright in the older patterns and not as a conventional sedge-type wing)
Hackle	White cock hackle

Various species of *Nectopsyche* occur in most parts of the USA.

THE HENRYVILLE

This fly was based on an earlier British sedge. It was a popular pattern on the trout streams of Pennsylvania. The original fly had a red body. The pattern itself dates back to the 1920s.

DRESSING

Hook	Mustad 94840 sizes 12–16
Thread	Green olive, or brown pre-waxed
Body	Light olive floss
Wing	Wood duck flanked by two strips of grey duck wing
Hackle	Palmered grizzle cock up the body and dark ginger at the head

Preston J. Jennings is recognised, along with Theodore Gordon, as being one of the influential pioneers of American fly fishing. His book, first published in 1935, is now considered to be a classic. It was titled quite simply *A Book of Trout Flies*. Among the fly patterns given in the book are a number of sedge imitations. It is interesting to note that he refers to the flies as sedges and not, as is now generally accepted in the USA, caddis. There is a sedge in the United States called *Psilotreta frontalis*, named by the early fly fishermen as the Dark Blue Sedge. In fact, the wing is grey so the term blue may well stem from the term 'blae' found in Scottish flies, or 'bloa' in British North Country patterns. Jennings gave a palmered imitation of this insect.

DARK BLUE SEDGE (*JENNINGS*)

Dark Blue Sedge

DRESSING

Hook	Mustad 94840 sizes 10–12
Thread	Brown pre-waxed
Body	Brown seal's fur
Rib	Fine gold wire
Hackle	Palmered rusty-blue-dun, white cock hackle at the head

KING RIVER CADDIS

This fly still appears in many of the fly catalogues of the major suppliers. It was created by Bus Buszec and can be used to imitate a wide number of mottled-wing caddis flies.

DRESSING

Hook	Mustad 94840 sizes 10–16
Thread	Black pre-waxed
Body	Brown fur dubbing, natural or synthetic
Wing	Mottled turkey
Hackle	Brown cock hackle

The American Grannom (*Brachycentrus americanus* or *B. fuliginosus*) is, as its name suggests, a very similar fly to our own *B. subnubilus*. J. Edson Leonard, author of the book *Flies*, gives a pattern for this sedge and also for the the Green Caddis (*Rhyacophila*). Both are tied in the traditional sedge manner.

American Grannom

AMERICAN GRANNOM

DRESSING

Hook	Mustad 94840 sizes 12–14
Thread	Green pre-waxed
Body	Yellowish-brown fur, natural or synthetic
Wing	Brown mallard
Hackle	Grizzle cock dyed ginger
Antennae	Wood duck

GREEN CADDIS

DRESSING

Hook	Mustad 94840 size 10
Thread	Green pre-waxed
Body	Raffia, dyed grass-green
Wing	Dark brown mottled turkey
Hackle	Olive cock hackle
Antennae	Ginger hackle fibres

The next fly is a popular pattern across the United States and well into Canada and Alaska. I have also seen it in the fly boxes of many British anglers. It can best be described as a fancy broad-spectrum fly. When fished on the surface it can represent a large sedge. It is also fished as a wet pattern to represent whatever the angler chooses; it is that sort of fly. I refer to the Hornberg. The originator was Frank Hornberg from Wisconsin. In recent years a number of darker versions have made their appearance.

THE HORNBERG

Hornberg

DRESSING

Hook	Mustad 38941 long shank sizes 8–12
Thread	Black pre-waxed
Body	Flat silver tinsel
Wing	Yellow cock hackle fibres or yellow hair, flanked by grey mottled mallard feathers. Often the mallard tips are cemented together
Cheeks	Jungle cock (these are often omitted when the fly is to be used as a dry sedge)
Hackle	Two grizzle cock hackles

THE CADDIS BUCK

DRESSING

Hook	Mustad 94840 sizes 8–12
Thread	Brown or orange pre-waxed
Body	Orange seal's fur or substitute
Wing	Deer hair
Hackle	Palmered furnace

There are many black sedges in the United States, among them the Little Black Sedge (*Chimarra aterrima*). The following pattern was used to imitate this.

Little Black Sedge

LITTLE BLACK CADDIS

DRESSING

Hook	Mustad 94840 sizes 12–16
Thread	Black pre-waxed
Body	Black seal's fur or similar
Wing	Coot or dyed goose
Hackle	Black or dark furnace

MODERN AMERICAN PATTERNS

The above flies are a representative sample of the many traditional sedge flies to be found in the USA. Recent research and certainly a greater awareness of the caddis as an important food source for trout, has spawned a wealth of intelligent fly patterns from the fly dressers of America. Many of these innovative patterns are in current use in the UK, and I have also seen their effect on many of the latest European flies.

In recent years two books on the caddis have influenced fly fishermen worldwide. These are *The Caddis and the Angler* by Solomon & Leiser, and the encyclopedic work *Caddis Flies* by Gary LaFontaine. Both these books should be on the shelves of the serious caddis angler and fly dresser. The following fly patterns are ones that I have used with success on rivers and stillwater in the UK. They are fun to tie.

CHUCK CADDIS

DRESSING

Hook	Mustad 94838 sizes 10–16
Thread	Light brown pre-waxed
Body	Mixed hare's mask and opossum
Wing	Woodchuck guard hair
Hackle	Two brown cock and grizzle cock

The spent or dying caddis can be represented by a fly called the Delta Caddis. The pattern was created by Larry Solomon. It can be tied up in varying sizes and in various colours to match the natural sedges found on the water. The wings are hackle points set at an angle of about 45 degrees.

DELTA CADDIS

Delta Caddis

DRESSING

Hook	Mustad 94840 sizes 10–16
Thread	Olive pre-waxed
Body	Olive fur, natural or synthetic
Wing	Grey hen hackle tips
Hackle	Brown cock hackle

BLACK DELTA CADDIS

DRESSING

Hook	Mustad 95840 sizes 10–16
Thread	Black pre-waxed
Body	Black fur, natural or synthetic
Wing	Black hen hackles
Hackle	Black cock hackle

Most species of caddis fly can be imitated in this style.

Another series of caddis, which is extremely popular on both sides of the Atlantic, is the Elk Hair Caddis. This pattern, I believe, was created by the eminent fly tier Al Troth. It can be tied in a variety of body and hackle colours to suit the natural. I have found this pattern highly successful in Europe.

ELK HAIR CADDIS

DRESSING

Hook	Mustad 94840 sizes 10–18
Thread	Brown pre-waxed
Body	Olive synthetic dubbing
Wing	Natural elk body hair
Hackle	Palmered brown cock
Head	The roots of the wing clipped to form the head

Darrel Martin of Tacoma, Washington State is one of the most meticulous fly dressers I know. His book, *Fly Tying Methods*, is a classic, and details many of his fly-tying skills. He writes with feeling, and illustrates his own work with detailed drawings. I envy his many skills, among which is his fly-tying ability. The following pattern is one of his.

MARSEDGE (*DARREL MARTIN*)

DRESSING

Hook	Mustad 94840 sizes 12–20
Thread	Brown pre-waxed
Body	Synthetic fur blend in the following colours depending on the sedge species: grey, black, dark green
Wing	Folded oak turkey trimmed to shape
Hackle	Grizzle or cree cock hackle
Antennae	Wood duck fibres

The natural sedge, which flutters above the surface of the water, has been imitated by many types of artificial fly. The following patterns, called Fluttering Caddis, were conceived by Leonard Wright and given in his book, *Fishing the Dry Fly as a Living Insect*. The patterns must be twitched and activated to simulate the behaviour of the real insect (see Palu's method on the Uneč in Chapter 11).

RED FLUTTERING SEDGE

DRESSING

Hook	Mustad 94840 sizes 12–14
Thread	Brown pre-waxed
Body	Cock pheasant tail fibres
Rib	Fine gold wire
Wing	Mink guard hairs or brown hackle fibres
Hackle	Brown cock hackle

Tied on smaller hooks down to size 20, and with a slightly darker body, the pattern is known as the Small Brown Fluttering Sedge.

There are a number of different colour variations in the Fluttering sedge series: tan, black, ginger, etc.

Mention has already been made of Gary LaFontaine and his major contribution to our knowledge of the Trichoptera. His Dancing Caddis patterns are yet another unique addition to the fly wallets of the fly fisherman. For this series of flies LaFontaine uses the unusually shaped Swedish Dry Fly Hook produced by Partridge of Redditch. By altering the colour of the materials used, most caddis species can be copied by this style of fly.

DANCING CADDIS

Dancing Caddis

DRESSING

Hook	Partridge Swedish Dry sizes 10–16
Thread	Black pre-waxed
Body	Thin synthetic dubbing of the desired colour to suit the natural being imitated
Wing	Deer body hair matched for colour with ·the natural sedge
Hackle	Cock hackle to match the insect

The main colour patterns for the Dancing Caddis are as follows:

THE BROWN AND YELLOW

Yellow body, speckled deer-hair wing, light brown hackle.

BROWN AND GREEN

Olive-brown body, speckled deer-hair wing, cree cock hackle.

DARK GREY

Mixed grey and brown fur body, grey deer hair, brassy dun hackle.

GINGER

Cream body, brown deer-hair wing, ginger cock hackle.

La Fontaine gives a whole range of secondary colour combinations.

The Large Orange Sedge (*Dicosmoecus* sp.) has been imitated by many artificial flies. The following is as good as any.

THE LARGE ORANGE SEDGE

DRESSING

Hook	Mustad 94840 sizes 6–8
Thread	Orange pre-waxed
Body	Orange synthetic dubbing
Wing	Natural bucktail tan colour
Hackle	Two, palmered orange and grizzle cock

There are a number of patterns used across America, and in the UK for that matter, which, on the face of it, do not look very much like sedges but have been found to be excellent flies during a hatch of caddis. The popular Adams dry fly is such an imitation, even though the wings are set upright. The famous Humpy or Goofus Bug is another such fly, and I have no doubt that many of the Wulff series of hairwings are taken by the trout as caddis. The following pattern is another used with some success during the hatch of sedge.

Vermont Caddis

THE VERMONT CADDIS

DRESSING

Hook	Mustad 94840 sizes 10–16
Thread	Grey pre-waxed
Tail	Grizzle hackle fibres tied short (optional)
Body	Mixed hare's ear and Australian possum
Hackle	Mixed brown and grizzle cock (two cree can be used instead)

This fly is sometimes called the Vermont Hare's Ear, and the hackles are sometimes clipped.

The fly patterns given in the last three chapters should be more than enough to give the reader some idea as to the numbers and styles of fly that are available to imitate the caddis fly in its winged state. I make no claims as to which is the best pattern; on their day they all have their moments and I would not like to choose a supreme champion among them. All I can say is that I have had fish on most of them.

CHAPTER THIRTEEN

FISHING THE ADULT SEDGE

For me, the sight of the first sedge fluttering bravely above the surface of the water is the harbinger of good times to come as far as my fishing is concerned. I think only the sight of a good mayfly hatch stirs my fishing soul as much and sends that tingle of anticipation right down to my finger tips. It is an anticipation born out of experience; a certain knowledge that even if the trout have been ignoring the delicate olives or allowing the veritable clouds of chironomids to pass them by, it is going to be a very blind or water-weary trout that will ignore such a tasty morsel as a sedge. Even if the trout have been feeding with gay abandon on other creatures, they will quite often change once a hatch of sedge gets underway.

I remember fishing on such an occasion. Mayflies had been hatching in veritable clouds; it was a hatch of dreams. Female mayflies joined these newborn flies and descended to the surface to lay their eggs. It was a river of intense activity, with the fish playing their part by rising to the duns that floated like stately galleons down the river, and to the spinners, wings outstretched as though crucified in the surface film. Then, after about an hour, the rise changed. The trout refused to look at our mayfly patterns, for large sedges had started to make their appearance. Alas, when the realisation of that fact eventually dawned on this tired angler it was too late. Darkness came down like a soft blanket to cover the river. I slowly waded out of the stream's flow and reached the bank tired but a little wiser. 'Next time," I said to myself, 'I will remember.' I now hope that I will once more find myself on such a river during the same sort of insect activity and have the satisfaction of changing my fly to suit the change in the diet of the trout, if and when it occurs, and with sufficient time left to take the odd fish before all the activity becomes cloaked by night.

The adult sedge is a very important fly both on rivers and on stillwater. There are many large waters where the mayfly hatches are either meagre or non-existent, but a hatch of the more water-tolerant sedge can be relied upon to provide good sport during the balmy evenings of the summer months and quite often throughout the whole day.

FISHING THE SEDGE ON STILLWATER

Fernworthy Reservoir lies like a liquid jewel set in forest green amidst the wilderness of Dartmoor. It is a water I have fished for over twenty years and it is possibly my favourite reservoir for a number of reasons. Unlike some of the more modern manmade waters, Fernworthy retains a certain primitive feel about it, as though it was not created by man at all but had always been there. If it were not for the granite dam, which guards one end like the walls of a Norman keep, you could believe that you were fishing a wild Scottish loch, left by the melting snows of the Ice Age. Those of you who like a little history to accompany your fishing will find it alongside this reservoir.

The first people to tread the spongy turf were the hunter gatherers who stalked the animals in the wooded valley of the River Taign. All they left behind was the odd scrap of worked flint to show that they had been there. After these primitive workers of stone came the Beaker people. Driving their animals ahead of them, they had followed the river that snaked its way to the high ground, before coming to the place we now call Fernworthy. Here they stayed, finding enough pasture for their few animals, fish in the rivers for the taking, blue berries to woad their children's lips and blue stone to change their copper to workable bronze. In this small valley of mists they made their homes. Today the granite stone circles of their houses and animal pens, still lying alongside the water, bear witness to their sojourn.

The streams that feed the reservoir rise in the wetness of the moor and because of this they tend to be acidic, so that the insect life found in them and in the reservoir itself tends to be fairly sparse. Additional flushes of acid water, leached from the forestry that surrounds the reservoir, do nothing for the well-being of this water. The fish in Fernworthy always appear to be hungry because of the low levels of aquatic food. They come readily to a fly fished on the top and are always on the lookout for terrestrial food like small beetles blown from the surrounding heather. I have seen sporadic hatches of summer duns from time to time, but too sparse to be of notable significance. So when the sedges make their appearance, one can safely say they are not ignored; the sedge, along with a small green midge, are important items in the diet of the Fernworthy trout.

I have got to admit that the sedge hatches at Fernworthy cannot in any way be described as prolific, but they do appear in sufficient numbers to interest the ever-hungry trout. I chose this wild reservoir as a scenario because it was the last stillwater I fished, using the sedge, at the end of the 1987 season, and there were a couple of lessons to be learnt during that particular trip, which can apply to all stillwaters, whether natural or manmade.

The day was dull. Rain hung in the air like wet muslin; a fine wetting rain that felt like wet perspiration on the face but was soft enough not to dampen my spirits. Although Fernworthy provides excellent bank fishing, on that particular day I chose to fish from a boat. Like anglers everywhere, I have my favourite spots on most waters–areas where I have had fish. It may be due to some natural reason, like a weedy area where insects and fish congregate, or some hidden contour beneath the water like a shelving bank or an old winding gulley of a lost ditch or stream. Perhaps it may even be due to the confidence factor; the same sort of confidence that makes a favourite fly work when no other fly will. You have caught good fish there once, so of course you are going to catch them there again, given the same set of circumstances, or so you hope.

I rowed across the main body of the water to the opposite bank and moved the boat towards the granite dam. At this place the bank slopes gently down into the water. There is a bottom of worn granite and quartz sand with a few time- and weather-worn grey boulders resting hump-backed out of the water. A little weed grows in this area and I have often taken fish on both wet and dry flies quite close to the edge. The wind, for a change, was not strong. It blew gently over the shoulder and towards the bank, thus making the fishing comfortable. It is only a small point, but if you are comfortable then, inevitably, you tend to fish better and be more aware of what is going on in the water around you. In more turbulent conditions it is not so easy to observe the subtleties of a trout's rise, or see what insects are on the water.

The first thing I noticed as I drifted slowly down the bank, was the fact that trout were rising within a foot or two of the edge and, furthermore, they were taking a small yellowy-brown sedge. I was not certain whether these sedges were newly hatched or were female sedges returning to oviposit, but certainly the trout appeared to be taking surface flies and not the sub-surface pupae. I watched the fish patrol up and down the length of the bank and make darting sorties right into the edge to take these small fluttering sedges. I put on a size 14 dry Red Sedge, cast this fly right onto the bank and waited for the fish to return to the area. As the fish swirled a little distance from my fly, I jerked the fly into the water and moved it about a foot. The result was an instant take and a brown trout of just over 1 lb (454 g) was duly landed. Had I chosen to fish from the bank that day and not from the boat, I would have approached the situation in the same way. As the fish were feeding close to the bank it would then have been necessary to stand well back from the water's edge and cast across the dry ground, with only a yard or so of leader lying in the water. When the trout appeared, a jerk back on the line would activate the little sedge fly and the result would be the same — a fooled fish. The rule that is paramount in all fishing is to look first. The unobservant might well have fallen into the usual reservoir trap and stepped boldly out in waders, with water lapping at the thighs, in order to try to cast into infinity, while the fish were, in fact, feeding behind the intrepid angler. Emphasis is placed on the word was, for in the circumstances that I found that day on Fernworthy the foraging fish would thus have been forced out of their feeding lane and well away from the bank, ending any sport for other anglers who had shown more common sense and had stood well back from the water's edge.

Bewl Water, my favourite 'big' water, has a perennial problem with weed. I say 'problem' and so it is for the bank angler and, of course, for the reservoir management who have to employ expensive weed-cutting machinery to overcome it, but it is no problem for the trout. Far from it, for they find these extensive weedy areas a veritable larder. They forage around the edges and into the weed zone itself after a wide variety of aquatic creatures such as *Corixa*, beetles, small fry and, of course, the ubiquitous sedge. Time and time again I have taken fish on a dry sedge from such places by drifting in close to the bank. (Because of the weed the boat angler is not disturbing any bank anglers for they are unable to fish in these weedy zones.) Often the fish have been bigger than normal, with a fair proportion of brown trout coming to the fly. The same sort of tactics are employed as described on Fernworthy; casting the bushy sedge onto the weed patch itself (trusting to providence that you do not get caught up, or by using a LaFontaine Dancing Caddis with the upturned hook) and pulling the fly off at the first sign of a feeding trout in the vicinity. In areas of fairly intense activity it pays to anchor up the boat at a safe distance, but within easy casting, and wait for the fish to show themselves. Sooner or later one will rise in front of you and the rest should be a foregone conclusion.

Stillwater trout behave in a different manner from those living in streams and rivers. They are more adventurous, they have the whole of the water to travel in, and rarely do they take up fixed feeding positions. Rainbows, for example, tend to shoal and will travel between two points, back and forth along the whole length of one bank, for example, or round and round in a bay. A jutting point between two such bays is a good place for a bank angler, for here he is able to intercept such shoaling fish as they follow the contours of the bank. The brown trout seem to be a little more conservative in their travelling. They tend to lurk in deeper water when not feeding, moving into the shallower areas as the light starts to fade. This is the time of the 'Waked' sedge.

A few years ago I happened to be fishing a medium-sized reservoir in the Weald of Kent. Called Bough Beech, it is situated midway between Sevenoaks and Edenbridge. The day was punctuated with the odd fish, all of them rainbows coming to a variety of flies, both nymph and lure. As daylight slid into darkness, trout became more active on the surface as chironomid midges clouded the reservoir. These surface-feeding trout were proving difficult as they were completely ignoring my team of chironomid pupae. I brought my line in and changed the flies to a large bushy 'wake' sedge which I dosed with a liberal quantity of floatant. I cast this hairy fly as far as I was able and left it to float for a short while. Then, by retrieving in long steady pulls, I waked the sedge back towards the bank. It took three pulls on the line before the rod was almost snatched from my hand by the take of a good fish. There was no frantic splashing, no leap in the air as is typical of a fit rainbow. This was a deep and steady, diving pull, the determined fight of a dogged brown trout. A couple of runs and a few dives later, I ultimately netted a beautiful brown trout close to 3 lb (1.36 kg).

This waked fly method is a very successful ploy for evening fishing on lake or reservoir. The action of the artificial emulates the behaviour of a newly hatched large sedge, such as a Caperer, which usually pauses for a short moment after emerging and then, in a helter skelter of untidy limbs, skitters towards the bank, creating quite a disturbance on the surface and accompanied by a distinct wake. This method reinforces the theory that one should fish the artificial as close to the behaviour of the natural as possible. In short, fish the fly as a living insect.

A similar method can be employed from a boat in the main body of the water. This can best be described as 'the intercept method'. This relies once more on observation; this time of the feeding path of the fish. The fly is more or less cast across this path at about 90 degrees, left to bob on its own until the approach of the fish, and then pulled across this feeding line. This method almost guarantees a caught fish. The intercept method can be employed from both a static and a drifting boat.

Another ploy which I have tried in the past on stillwaters is 'the two-fly method' and its variations. The first variation I discovered more or less by accident. It was during the cranefly time in late September, a period of great surface activity on such reservoirs as Bewl, when big rainbows that have sulked in the quiet depths rise to the occasion to take the spindle-shanked daddy longlegs as it tumbles in the surface film. Here I tend to fish a dry cranefly pattern on the point and, on a dropper about 5 ft away, a smaller sedge pattern. I have found that fish can be taken on both flies in equal numbers. Even though the trout have definitely been tempted to the surface by craneflies, such is their love of the sedge they will often turn from the cranefly and take the smaller sedge pattern bobbing ahead of it.

The second variation uses two sedge patterns and is generally used from a moving, rather than an anchored, boat. The first sedge on the point can either be an established sedge fly not treated with floatant, or a traditional wet sedge pattern. The second sedge on the dropper is treated so that it does float. Casting ahead of the moving boat, the flies are drawn back with the dry sedge bobbing the surface and the wet sedge skating back just under the surface film. Trout will be taken on both flies.

Traditional 'dapping' methods can be adopted by using heavily palmered sedge flies instead of the more usual dapping patterns. The sedge fly is ideally suited to the silk blow line style of dapping, for the natural insect behaves in very much the same way as a bobbing dapping fly. With a good steady wind and a fair lop to the wave, dapping can be a very effective method of taking trout. It must be true to say that the usual dapping flies are the mayfly and the cranefly, but there is nothing at all to stop you using a large, heavily hackled sedge for the same purpose.

The long-established 'loch style' can be adapted to fishing the sedge by using a sedge pattern on the bob fly and the traditional wets on the point and intermediate dropper. As stated earlier, it is my belief that many of our lake wet flies are, in fact, reasonable imitations of sedge flies or sedge pupae.

The one method I have not yet mentioned is what I like to term the 'sandwich method'. This is a very basic method, for if you cast out your sedge pattern and leave it to bob on the surface as you partake of a sandwich and a cup of coffee, then you can almost be sure of a take at the precise moment of biting into the sandwich or pouring the coffee from the flask. It is almost uncanny how often this situation occurs.

FISHING THE SEDGE ON RIVERS AND STREAMS

Although the term stillwater is not precisely correct, for there is always a water or a wind-motivated movement to drift your fly slowly, an angler still has to provide most of the action of his artificial sedge by the way he retrieves and uses his fly line. On rivers it is totally different. Here there is too much movement in the water for the purposes of fishing and the angler spends his time trying to arrest the subsequent movement of his fly in order that it should appear to the fish like a natural insect. On rivers presentation is of prime importance. The rules I try to abide by are as follows: *observation*, *match the hatch* and *presentation*. If it is possible to adhere to these three principles, then success is not long in coming, although I have to admit nothing is ever cut and dried when it comes to fishing the fly.

The trout in rivers behave differently to those in stillwater. In rivers they tend to be territorial, taking up a station in the river where they are comfortable, where energy is conserved and where a steady stream of food is brought to them, rather than having to forage over long distances to seek their meals. They also have another station, a place of safety, a bolt hole at times of disturbance or fright, or a place of rest. These non-feeding areas could be in the depths of a pool, under a bank overhang, under stones or amidst a tangle of submerged roots. They do not often feed in these bolt holes, but move into their feeding stations at the appropriate time. On rivers for most of the time we will be fishing to rising fish – fish we can see. Then it becomes a question of how we present the fly to the fish? This is dictated by the lie of the fish and the topography of the river. It may be easier to fish upstream or quite the reverse. Sometimes speculative fishing of the dry fly is necessary when there are no obvious signs of a feeding trout. Our sedge pattern is then used to tempt a trout to rise, and the fly is therefore cast into areas where trout should be. Knowledge of the river and experience certainly help in such circumstances.

The River Darent rises in the hills around the small town of Westerham. It meanders through the lush Darent valley and eventually slips into the Thames at Dartford creek. I have fished this small chalk stream for nearly 25 years and although the fishing is not as good now as in the last century, due to various polluting factors and that insidious bain of rivers in the south, water abstraction, there are stretches which are stocked by the various clubs which control its length.

There is a quiet portion of the river which, for the sake of this chapter, I will call Kingfisher Pool. I could well have called it One-Eyed Pool, for a number of years ago I decided to investigate a small hole in the opposite bank. Wading across the stream I pulled myself up and peered down the hole. Like a flash a kingfisher shot out in a blur of shining blue and orange and all but took my eye with it. These days I show a little more caution and no longer peer down holes in the bank. As you will see from the sketch, a tree hugs the corner of the pool and beneath its shelter the water is at its deepest. Quite often good fish hide amidst the untidy tangle of roots and under the flotsam of dead branches and twigs carried there by the stream.

I cast my fly into the pool but no interest was taken in it as it swung around in the slow current, so it was time for a think. I changed the weighted nymph to a small grey sedge and cast into the fast water ahead of the pool, hoping that the fly would be carried naturally into the pool. It had not travelled more than a foot or two when it was taken by a fighting rainbow which I duly landed. I had misread the situation. The small pool by the tree was, in fact, the trout's haven, its place of refuge when frightened, its resting area from the rough and tumble of the stream. The faster water above was its true feeding zone. I had discovered this by accident, but since that time I have often taken fish ahead of the deeper water, having learned the lesson that I should have looked first. I was fortunate on that occasion and caught my fish, but it was more by luck than design. Had I perhaps waited and observed the water for a while I might have appreciated the true nature of the picture. It is surprising how often this situation of fast runs and deeper pools is repeated on other rivers that I have fished, and how often the trout have been feeding in the fast water and resting in the safety of the deeper holes. Every so often, though, I must admit I have found fish rising in the deeper water, but these have always indicated their presence by the rises themselves.

THE DRAG CONFRONTATION

The biggest problem facing a fly fisherman on moving water is the problem of line drag. This pull of the faster currents on the fly line

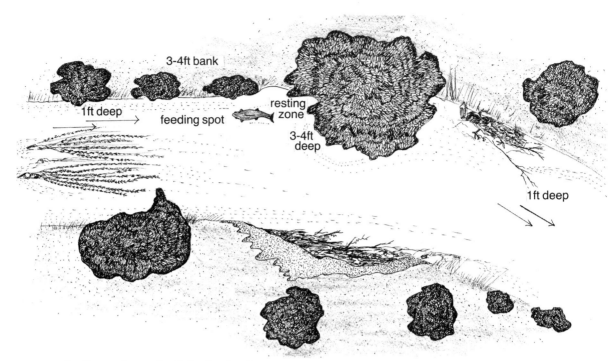

3-4ft bank

1ft deep

feeding spot

resting zone

3-4ft deep

1ft deep

Kingfisher Pool

moves the fly at the end of the leader in a most unnatural manner. The confrontation between the angler and adverse river currents is lessened by mending the line or by casting in such a way as to make your fly line land in the water in a series of tight loops or curves. This, in effect, premends the line and slows up the progress of the fly. There are times, however, when an element of drag to the fly actually helps when fishing the adult sedge.

Let me explain. If you are fishing your artificial in a dead drift, by casting upstream and across and mending the line in order to keep your sedge fly moving in a natural manner, as its progress commences downstream and acceleration sets in, there is a brief period when the fly starts to move quickly, dragged into the faster current by the fly line. Quite often a trout will take at that precise moment, for the fly is emulating the behaviour of some natural sedges that have floated down with the current for a while before skittering across the surface in order to take off or to reach the safety of the bank. Bearing this in mind, it often pays to fish out the first element of the dragged fly before lifting off and recasting.

DRY DOWN, WET BACK

Mention has been made earlier of the River Krka in Slovenia. It is truly a river of the sedges. I have fished many rivers and streams but know of no other river where the trout feed all day on the variety of different species found on this Slovenian chalk stream. I had been fishing the slow moving typical chalk-stream stretch with a dead drift dry fly. My friend Dr Bozidar Voljč had chosen to work his flies in the faster water below the mill race, so I took a little time off to watch his technique. He stood waist-deep in the water, casting his dry sedge a little to the right and downstream. A few yards of fly line were fed through the rings in order to keep the fly floating naturally. When the point of no return was reached and drag began to take over, he retrieved his fly by short pulls so that, in fact, he was now fishing a wet fly. This method of fishing the sedge on rivers can be very rewarding. It is reminiscent of methods used on British West Country streams. The fly starts out as a dry pattern but, after being swamped by the bubbling troubled water, its use is continued as a wet fly until a new fly is tied on or the existing pattern is dried off.

The question of how a wet sedge pattern can prove effective on streams and rivers is answered by the behaviour of the natural sedge itself. In many sedge species the ovipositing females actually dive into the water and swim down to the bottom to lay their eggs. As they dive, the insects are cocooned in a bubble of air trapped by the natural hairs found on their bodies. This return for egg-laying purposes often occurs at a time when fresh sedges are hatching. It has been known for the trout to feed more on these egg layers in preference to the newly hatching flies. This may well be due to the fact that these females, laden with eggs, offer a more tasty meal for the trout. So it is always worth having one or two patterns to imitate this stage in the sedge's life cycle. Perhaps one of the best ones I have used was sent to me by Roman Moser of Austria. He refers to it as the Diving Caddis.

DIVING CADDIS

Moser's Diving Caddis

DRESSING

Hook	Mustad 94840 or similar sizes 8–14
Thread	Brown pre-waxed
Body	Brown or green seal's fur or substitute
Wings	Teased out polypropylene mixed with Crystal Hair (this is a fine tinsel hair used for all types of wings. It comes in a wide range of colours.) For the sedges the brown shade is ideal. The tinsellated wing shimmers in the water, not unlike the real insect clothed as it is in bubbles of air

I mentioned earlier how I found the traditional Invicta and its variant, the Silver Invicta, to be successful on rivers. This may well be for the reason I have just given, that the trout view the flies as egg-laying females.

THE CHANGE OF DIRECTION DRAG

For many years I had the good fortune to fish a number of stretches of the River Torridge in Devon. I caught my first salmon on this river so I will always have a soft spot for this Devon stream. For many years the Torridge, along with its twin, the River Taw, was justly famed for the runs of both salmon and sea-trout. In more recent times various forms of pollution have taken their toll; agricultural and sewage effluents appear to be the main culprits. I gather that steps are now being taken to remedy the deplorable state that the river has fallen into. Let us hope it is not too late and that the river once more returns to its former glory as the haunt of dippers and kingfishers, of salmon and sea-trout, to be a place where perhaps the descendants of Henry Williamson's Tarka will once again play in the crystal stream.

Late in the season I fished one particular stretch for two days. I had waded the length of the beat, casting to my left and casting to my right at fish that were rising. Most turned out to be small finger-marked salmon parr that did not know any better. I came to a bend in the stream where a large tree sheltered the river. It looked like a place where trout could lie comfortably out of the sun, in water that was about 2 ft deep and moving fairly quickly. Where I was wading the water got progressively deeper. Fishing across to this potential holding spot was going to pose difficulties. I passed on by as I saw nothing rise in the vicinity. I had not gone more than 10 yd when I heard a fish splash in what I thought was a good sedge rise. I looked over my shoulder to see slowly vanishing rings in the water beneath the tree. I sidled my way back in an endeavour to cast to this rising fish. My sedge fly sailed out under the tree and into the shade where it received no response at all. I cast once more, but again nothing. Then, with a resounding plop and a perfect set of concentric rings, an acorn fell from the sheltering oak. Yes, for ten minutes I had been fishing for acorns. I looked around to make certain nobody had witnessed my embarrassment, smiled to myself and moved on.

A little further downstream I saw some real fish rise. The only way I could cast to them was directly downstream. This I did, allowing my fly to float casually over the area of activity. It did not work, so I cast again and once more my little sedge did not prompt a

Day of the Acorn

rise. I pulled back on the fly line so that the fly skittered along the surface, then, by angling my rod, I let it drift down on another line. The fly was taken immediately. I tried this method again; drifting down, a slight drag or skitter back across the surface, then a drift once more on a new tack. This took the other fish that had been rising in that corner. To the trout this must have appeared as a natural insect floating down then struggling upstream against the flow, giving up and once more floating back downstream. Whatever the truth of the matter, the ploy worked and has continued to work on many other rivers since that day on the Torridge, a day I always recall as the Day of the Acorns.

THE UPSTREAM DRY

I suppose that to creep up on the quarry as it faces upstream is the most effective way of fishing a dry fly. However, care must be taken not to line the fish and also, when wading, great care must be taken in not sending a bow wave up ahead of you to disturb the fish. On some British chalk streams this is the only method allowed, and then usually from the bank. The advice I was given was to fish with a short line and keep a low profile; keep concealed as much as possible and watch the obvious things like shadow; disturb the water as little as possible.

THE SEDGE AND THE FLOOD

I was shown this next method of taking fish in adverse conditions on the famed, fast flowing Sava river in Yugoslavia, by a French writer who writes for both Japanese and European magazines. Georges Lenzi and I arrived at the river only to find it in fast flowing flood. To me it was unfishable, but my French friend said we should have some good sport. I said nothing and put his optimism down to some strange Gallic quirk. 'All the fish that were in the middle of the river are now close into the banks,' said Georges. I agreed that this was highly likely as I had just witnessed a 20-ft tree come shooting down the river like a sledge on the Cresta Run. 'We will creep up the bank and find the quiet places.' Georges continued. I nodded agreement, more in a feeling of *entente cordiale* than as a positive response to his obvious enthusiasm. The river twisted and turned in a multitude of conflicting currents, but close into the bank there were small areas of apparent calm water, as though a spoonful of oil had been poured there to quell the turbulence.

Georges cast his fly a few yards ahead into one of these flat patches. The fly sat pert on the surface for a second or so and then a silvered rainbow rose, took the fly and sped off as though seeking the sanctuary of the Adriatic. This was repeated in every quiet-water corner and each time a fish obliged by rising to the occasion. Even a slightly obtuse Welshman was convinced and now, whenever I meet similar conditions, I try this method using a small light-coloured sedge. I find the sedge to be an ideal pattern for this type of fishing, for it floats well, stands up high on the water, and can be seen easily by the trout and, perhaps more important, by me.

THE EMERGING SEDGE

I have always thought the emerging sedge pattern to be an in between stage. It is neither fished like the pupal patterns given in earlier chapters, nor is it fished totally as a dry fly. It can be termed as a 'film' fly, a pattern to be fished within the surface film and not as a dry fly sitting pert on the surface. Buoyant materials, used in many of the modern emerger patterns, guarantee that the flies themselves behave in this desired fashion. For most of the time I fish emergers on a dead drift up and across the stream, or downstream with an additional feed of line through the rings to hold up the inevitable line drag.

THE SEDGE AND THE GRAYLING

The methods already described for taking trout will, of course, hold true for the grey lady of the stream, the grayling. The next two methods I have found to be very effective in taking grayling, and it goes without saying that they will also take trout. Earlier I mentioned the fact that most people who fished the River Uneč in Slovenia fished downstream. Since writing that I came to realise that for most of the time they were fishing for grayling, not trout. This should have been obvious to me, and as though to prove me wrong in my previous assumptions regarding this river, my wife caught a fine two lb (454 g) brown trout right in front of my very eyes by fishing a short line upstream.

I have spent more days on this chalk river than all my days on the Test and Itchen combined, and have noted many of the methods adopted by our Yugoslav brothers in fishing across and down for what is for them the king of fish, the grayling.

The first secret is not to cast a long line. The cast must be kept short, for the fish will rise just a few yards from the wading angler. One day I had gone downstream earlier and taken one or two fish and then I stopped fishing for a well-earned pipe of tobacco. I watched another angler follow me down, but without the same success, and then he gave up and joined me on the bank. As though to surrender to the river, he removed his fly vest and hung it on a bush. We chatted awhile before I ventured once more into the fast flowing stream. The fish seemed to be rising with more determination than before and I noticed a few brown sedges on the surface. My first few casts were ignored; my sedge bobbed on the surface unmolested – it was time to change my fly. I looked through my box and found a small brown flat-wing sedge which sat in the water with a much lower profile. In fact, it rested just in the surface film. Three casts with this fly brought three good grayling in quick succession. I do not know if the fish took the sedge as an emerger or as a spent sedge, all I know is that on that morning it was the most killing fly and method. It also prompted my fellow angler to don his fly vest once more and re-enter the fray.

Another method which I have found to work well, both in the UK and abroad, is the 'float and dunk' sedge. The fly is cast across and down to the rising fish and just before it arrives at the place where the fish is rising, a sharp jerk is imparted to the fly line so that the sedge dips below the surface. It is then that the fish usually takes.

The methods of fishing sedge patterns described in this book are the ones I have adopted over many years. I am not telling you that you should do the same, far from it, only that they work for me and could well do the same for you.

CHAPTER FOURTEEN

COLLECTING AND PHOTOGRAPHY

Over the last ten years or so I have given talks throughout the length and breadth of the UK to a wide variety of fishing clubs. During the usual question time I am inevitably asked how I took the photographs and what camera I use, etc. From this I assume that a fair proportion of anglers have an interest in this facet of our sport, although I know that most do not want to concern themselves with the intricacies of angling entomology or with the photographing of insects. However, this has always been part of my fishing experience, one that I have valued greatly, and I am sure that my subsequent fishing has improved through my recognition of the insects on the water. If we can glean a little knowledge regarding the insects we copy at the fly vice, by studying their behaviour, I feel we are going some considerable way to increasing our knowledge of the trout itself, for a trout's behaviour while feeding must be governed by the behaviour of its prey.

Insects are collected for two basic reasons. First, for closer identification at leisure, and second, for further study, perhaps in an aquarium. For many years I had such an aquarium, which gave me an endless source of interest and study. Whereas many of my friends had large aquariums with the very latest in filters and a myriad fine, multi-coloured tropical fish, mine had caddis larvae, shrimps, *Dytiscus* beetles and other aquatic insects. My only concession to fish was a few sticklebacks and minnows. I had recreated in my tank a mini-version of a pond. I must admit that occasionally there were problems, like the time my *Dytiscus* beetles decided they did not like this bubbling habitat and decided to migrate to aqueous pastures new. I found one whirling around in the plug hole of the sink; the other two, I fear, went quite literally round the bend. There was also a time when the newts I was studying decided to do their version of the great escape. Alas, they ended up in the vacuum cleaner. Most of the time, though, my aquarium proved extremely useful for observing freshwater life.

Because I was trying to recreate a habitat as close as possible to the real thing, I did not segregate the various species and I found I was suffering high predation losses. Until you have such an insight into what goes on under the water you would not credit how steeped in blood most of these creatures are. Many became the stuff of nightmares. So if you intend to study a particular species or group of insects, be careful what you put in the aquarium with them. Many of the caddis larvae, such as *Rhyacophila* or *Hydropsyche*, are voracious predators and are not averse to feeding on their own kind. The study can become a case of the survival of the fittest.

COLLECTING

Some form of net or nets is required for collecting nymphs and larvae, etc. I use a sturdy triangular net for grubbing in the silt and stones. The net portion is made from a strong hessian; more modern versions use stronger polypropylene. A seine net, made of two posts with fine white netting attached between them, is another way of collecting such aquatic creatures. The stones or gravel are stirred up in front of the net and any creatures dislodged are carried into the

Seine net

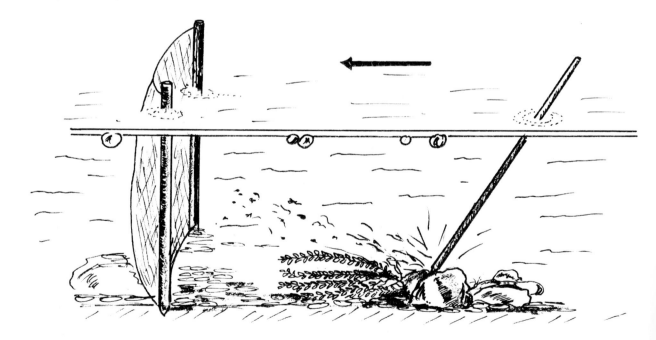

net by the current. For insects on the surface, a small net, similar to the type used by aquarists, can be quite useful for scooping up any winged insects. I also resort to a large butterfly net for catching insects on the wing. You will have to bear the odd jibe from fellow anglers as you gallop around the undergrowth, but after a while even they accept you as a harmless eccentric. Do not be surprised, however, if some of these sceptics start to help when the fishing gets a bit quiet. I also use the same net to sweep the bankside vegetation and capture any insects resting up out of the sun. For taking the insects back alive, for study, etc., small glass or plastic containers are essential. The lids must be perforated. I once found a company that was importing vast quantities of record-player styli. When they attached these to the main equipment, the little plastic pots they had been packed in were usually dumped. I persuaded them otherwise and ended up with about 3,000 very useful collecting pots.

Killing jar

For one reason or another it may be necessary to kill the odd specimen to keep for future reference. For this one needs a killing bottle. In the old days entomologists generally used potassium cyanide killing jars. I would not recommend such a killing medium. Being of a careless disposition I would more than likely kill myself along with the insects and probably the rest of my family at the same time. It is far better to employ one of the liquids now normally used for this purpose, such as ethyl acetate, trichloro-ethylene or even carbon tetrachloride, but even with these an element of care must be taken and they *must* be kept well out of reach of children and pets. I use a wide-mouthed screw- or cork-topped jar for this purpose, into which I have poured a layer of plaster of Paris. This dries into an absorbent pad which holds the killing liquid. Crushed up laurel leaves can also be used as a killing agent. Do not kill any insect if you do not have to. There can be no justification these days of collecting for collecting's sake; it should only be done for reference or for identification of the species. Photographic records are usually far more rewarding than serried ranks of pinned-out dried-up insect specimens. Whenever possible release any insect into a suitable environment after you have finished with it.

Collecting pot

Most species of sedge are attracted to light, and a very useful item of equipment for the serious student is a moth trap. For many years there was such a trap alongside the residential centre at Grafham Water, and it was quite surprising the number of sedges we caught in one night. My own moth trap was a powerful affair. When I switched it on in the garden for the first time, my neighbours thought that we were being visited by extra-terrestrials, but it did draw sedges from over half a mile away.

Those wishing to preserve larvae and or pupae should place the insects in a sealed container in a preserving fluid. This fluid is usually made up of a pure ethyl alcohol and ethyl acetate mixture, or sometimes a 2 per cent solution of formalin can also be used.

Finally we come to identification. As explained earlier this is not an easy exercise to undertake. It requires first and foremost a microscope and a lot of patience. I was fortunate in having the late David Jacques as a friend and colleague and he confirmed and identified all the specimens of sedges that I collected, thus relieving me of a lot of hard work. For this I shall always be in his debt. With a microscope and armed with the appropriate reference keys, etc., it is not impossible to identify the various species that make up the family Trichoptera. A solution of potassium hydroxide is generally used to help to expose the genitalia of the adult sedges.

PHOTOGRAPHY

Apart from the camera itself, the most essential thing required in photographing insects is patience. Wherever possible, I like to photograph my subjects in the field. I always feel the resultant pictures are more natural and, to a degree, more aesthetic if photographed this way. However, this does pose certain problems. It is rare for the insect to stay still. The photographer has to stalk the subject and become a hunter in the grass root jungle, hence the amount of patience required. To these obvious difficulties you can add a high percentage of film wastage or, to put it another way, I have a large number of slides of green leaves with insect legs departing stage left. Because they tend to be weak fliers, sedges are perhaps not as difficult as some other insect species to photograph, but they do have the annoying habit of running away, a feature they share with the stoneflies. I have to admit that it is easier to capture specimens and bring them indoors to photograph in an enclosed space where perhaps the end results would be more scientific.

It all depends on what you require the pictures for. If you require them purely as a photographic record, then this indoor photography is perhaps the best method to use. On the other hand, if they are to be used for illustrative purposes, for magazine, book or lecture work, then it is more pleasing on the eye to see the subjects in a natural setting, even though this poses the difficulties already mentioned. I think the photographer must use a little common sense when it comes to a particularly rare or uncommon species. To risk the escape of the sedge for the sake of art is a little foolish, and in

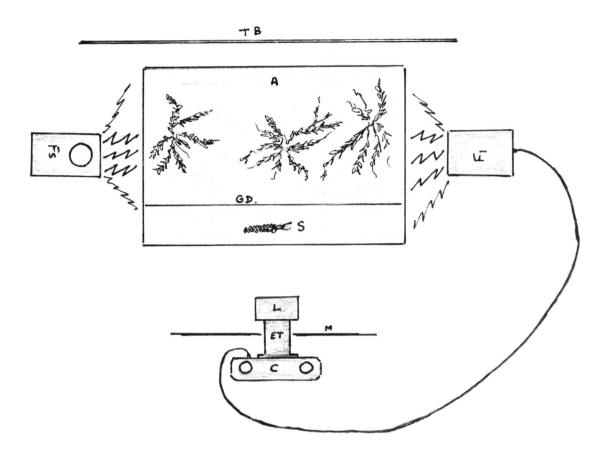

Photographing in Aquarium

A – aquarium
C – camera
Et – extension tube
Fl – electronic flash
Fs – electronic slave unit
ED – glass divider
TB – Tinted background
M – camera mask
S – subject

those circumstances I generally capture the specimen, photograph it where it cannot escape, and then release it in a suitable environment.

EQUIPMENT

The best and easiest camera to use for this macro-photography is a single lens reflex camera, or SLR for short. In this day and age there are a large number of models to choose from, many with all sorts of technical features. My advice to a beginner is to buy a simple basic model, for most of the time the macro operation is purely a manual one and therefore many of the complex features offered by some models are of limited use. They can also be confusing to the newcomer. For many years I used a very basic Praktica camera and was able to take many pictures that were subsequently published. I now use a Pentax ES model which has since been superseded many times by later designs. As this camera serves me well, however, I feel no need to change. I must admit that I cannot, in all honesty, say that my Pentax takes any better pictures than my original inexpensive German camera and, furthermore, I have a friend who takes equally good pictures using a very cheap Russian model. As with most things in life, it is not the camera but the man behind it that makes the good photograph.

For close-up photography a number of other items of equipment will be needed and must be considered as essential. First is a set of extension tubes. These are fitted between the camera and the lens. They usually came in a set of three and all three will give you a magnification of × 1 with a standard 50-mm lens. This is all you will need to photograph most sedges. The amount of light reaching the film is reduced by using extension tubes. On automatic cameras and automatic extension tubes, of course, this is registered on the built-in lightmeter and the camera adjusts itself accordingly. On manual cameras this has to be calculated and adjusted. In order to simplify things I found that by using an electronic flash and an aperture of f16, I was able to obtain tolerably good results with a reasonable depth of field.

Indoors, greater magnification can be achieved by fitting an extension bellows instead of tubes. I have, however, used both in *Photographing using electronic flash*

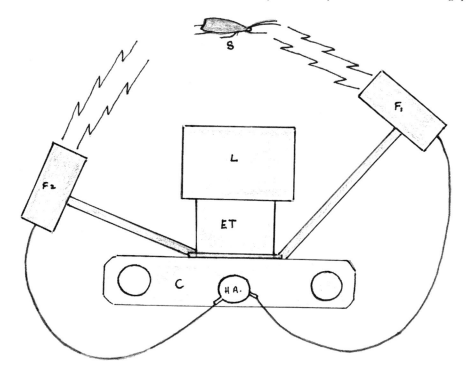

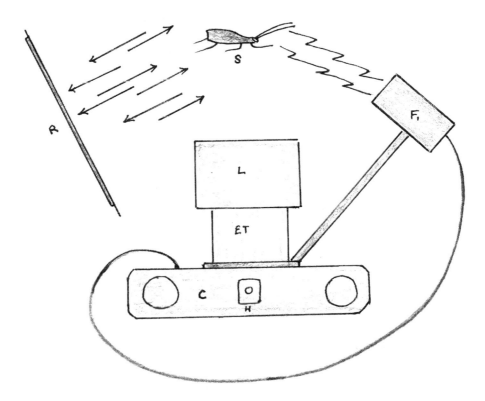

Photographing with flash

C – camera
ET – extension tubes
Fl – electronic flash
HA – hot shoe adapter
H – hot shoe
L – lens
R – reflector
S – subject

conjunction to achieve even greater magnification. In fact, when you get to this sort of situation you are in the realms of micro-photography. It is possible to purchase supplementary lenses that screw into the front of your standard lens. These will give you a magnification increase depending on the dioptre figure of the lens. When in doubt as to which to buy, ask an experienced shop assistant to advise you, but, as an example, a 1-dioptre lens will give you a magnification increase of 0.05, while one of 20 dioptres gives × 1 when using the standard 50-mm lens.

While it is possible to photograph insects when they are quiescent, by using available natural light it is far easier in the field to make use of the electronic flash, for the insects are seldom still when you want to photograph them. Special bars can be fixed to the camera to place the flash closer to the front of it in order to maximise the light on the subject. An additional small flash gun, triggered by a slave unit which fires the flash automatically when the other flash goes off, can also be useful. (This slave flash gun is not triggered by sunlight or by tungsten light.) A sheet of white paper or aluminium foil can also be used to concentrate light close to the subject or to enhance natural light.

I have nearly always used a hand-held camera for most of my field photography. I focus on the subject with a slight rocking motion until the insect is sharp and at that point I trigger the camera. For this I find a cable release to be important and also use a pistol grip to steady the camera.

Indoors it is possible to photograph using tungsten lighting, either by using a combination of flood lights or smaller lights, such as those used to illuminate microscope subjects. The only drawback to using this form of illumination is that the heat emitted by such floods can tend to harm the subject, plus the fact that one has to use special tungsten film. Outside a combination of flash and bright sunlight affords the best results.

For photographing larvae underwater, I resort to using what can best be described as a mini-aquarium which I construct out of glass and a U-form made out of clear polythene tubing about $\frac{3}{4}$ in in diameter. I place my light source above this mini-aquarium and photograph directly into it. Photographing into a larger aquarium can be done in a number of different ways by using a combination of electronic flash units and aluminium foil. The flash can be placed directly above the aquarium with foil sheets at both sides and a back sheet of pale blue or green. This back sheet enhances the overall coloration of the picture, giving the water a natural watery look. The subject can be isolated in the front of the aquarium by inserting a separate piece of glass. Flashes can be placed on each side of the aquarium and a foil sheet placed at an angle above it. The camera can be masked by a sheet of board with a central hole cut out to accept the lens. For this kind of photography a sturdy tripod is a decided advantage and again a cable release is essential.

MACRO-LENSES

These are special lenses designed for close-up photography; some zoom lenses also have a built-in macro capability. I use a macro-lens for the larger insects such as the biggest of the sedge species, butterflies, dragonflies and damsel flies. Like a standard lens, it can be used in conjunction with extension tubes, bellows and supplementary lenses. In fact, I have had very good results using my 100-mm macro-lens, with supplementary lenses, to photograph small artificial flies using tungsten lighting.

There is one system of lighting I have not mentioned which I also use from time to time both in and out of doors and that is a ring flash. This item of equipment is designed to encompass the lens with in circular flash unit and can be worked by batteries or directly from the mains. The drawbacks to this item are the fact that you have to carry a battery pack over your shoulder or attached to your belt, which can be a little cumbersome, there is a multiplicity of cables, which in my case always seem to get detached at the wrong moment, and, finally, the lighting tends to be a little flat and unnatural. By masking off a small portion of the ring with paper masking tape or a piece of white muslin, better-lit results can be obtained.

As with fishing, the insect stalker must be dressed in drab clothing to blend with the background. White shirts, etc., usually cause the insects to depart very rapidly. Even the pale area of a face can do this, so always keep your camera up to your face when approaching your subject.

FILM

Most people have their favourite make of film. When I first started photographing insects I used an Agfa CT18, 50ASA film or the equivalent Agfa Professional film. The results using these films were very good. They seemed to suit the subject matter which was inevitably photographed on green leaves. The film colour seemed to favour this green bias, unlike some other films which seemed to haze the slide in a blue bias. This may have been my imagination or my eyesight and colour appreciation, but I do not think so.

Recently I have used Agfa CT100 or Kodachrome 64. The low-speed films give very good results with electronic flash and the subjects are usually in sharp detail. The higher the film speed the more grainy is the result, but you do tend to get a softer, less fierce contrast.

For use with tungsten lighting the film I use is Kodak Ekta-chrome 160. You will notice that I refer only to slides and not prints. Slides are a more convenient medium for keeping a photographic record, for publishing, and for showing to a large number of people by means of a projector. Prints can be taken from the slides if you so desire.

A projector can also be used to show the natural wings of the sedge if you use glass slide mounts. The wing is placed in the mount and projected onto the screen. This can facilitate identification by wing venation. Slides can be stored in boxes made especially for this purpose. Each slide should be marked with the place and date where you photographed it, the correct scientific name of the sedge and, finally, your own name. Good slides should be mounted in glass slide mounts.

Roberts, *New Dictionary of Trout Flies*, Allen & Unwin 1986.
Robson, *Robson's Guide*, Beekay 1985.
Roskelly (ed.), *Flies of the North West*, Int. Emp. Fly. 1979.
Solomon and Leiser, *Caddis and the Angler*, Stackpole 1977.
Swisher and Richards, *Fly Fishing Strategy*, Crown 1975.
Veniard, *Fly Dressers' Guide*, A&C Black 1952.
Veniard, *Further Guide to Fly Dressing*, A&C Black 1964.
Veniard, *Reservoir and Lake Flies*, A&C Black 1970.
Walker, C.F. *Chalk Stream Trout Flies*, A&C Black 1953.
Walker, R. *Modern Fly Dressings*, Benn 1980.
Ward and Whipple, *Fresh water Biology*, Wiley 1945.
Whitlock, *Guide-to Aquatic Trout Food*, Nick Lyons 1982.
Williams, *Dictionary of Trout Flies*, A&C Black 1949.

USEFUL ADDRESSES

FLY & FISHING EQUIPMENT SUPPLIERS

Farlows of Pall Mall
5 Pall Mall
London SW1

Francesco Palu
33030 Campoformido
Via Silvio Pellico 44
Udine
Italy

Guy Plas
19320 Marcillac-La-Croisille
France

Marryat Interfly
Postfach 8031
Gasometerstrasse 23
Ch-8005 Zurich
Switzerland

Salmo
Apartado De Correos 53206
Madrid
Spain

Steff's Fluebinding
Skolevaenget 14
83100 Tranbjerg
Denmark

Tom Saville Ltd (mail order)
Unit 7 Salisbury Sq
Middleton Street
Nottingham NG7 2AB

Traun River Products
Hauptstrasse 6
D-8227 Siegsdorf
West Germany

NATURAL HISTORY EQUIPMENT SUPPLIER

Watkins & Doncaster Ltd
Four Throws
Hawkhurst
Kent

WHOLESALE FLY-DRESSING MATERIALS

Medway Feather Company
Brasenose Road
Gillingham
Kent
England

E. Veniard (Wholesale) Ltd
138 Northwood Road
Thornton Heath
Surrey
England

INDEX OF NATURAL
SEDGES

INDEX OF FLY PATTERNS

ADULT PATTERNS